IN THE CARQUINEZ WOODS

BRET HARTE

In the Carquinez Woods

Bret Harte

© 1st World Library, 2007
PO Box 2211
Fairfield, IA 52556
www.1stworldlibrary.com
First Edition

LCCN: 2007934086

Softcover ISBN: 978-1-4218-9623-6
Hardcover ISBN: 978-1-4218-9723-3
eBook ISBN: 978-1-4218-9523-9

Purchase *"In the Carquinez Woods"*
as a traditional bound book at:
www.1stWorldLibrary.com/purchase.asp?ISBN=978-1-4218-9623-6

1st World Library is a literary, educational organization
dedicated to:

- Creating a free internet library of downloadable ebooks

- Hosting writing competitions and offering book publishing
scholarships.

Interested in more 1st World Library books? contact:
literacy@1stworldlibrary.com
Check us out at: www.1stworldlibrary.com

1st World Library Literary Society

Giving Back to the World

"If you want to work on the core problem, it's early school literacy."

- James Barksdale, former CEO of Netscape

"No skill is more crucial to the future of a child, or to a democratic and prosperous society, than literacy."

- Los Angeles Times

"Literacy... means far more than learning how to read and write... The aim is to transmit... knowledge and promote social participation."

- UNESCO

"Literacy is not a luxury, it is a right and a responsibility. If our world is to meet the challenges of the twenty-first century we must harness the energy and creativity of all our citizens."

- President Bill Clinton

"Parents should be encouraged to read to their children, and teachers should be equipped with all available techniques for teaching literacy, so the varying needs and capacities of individual kids can be taken into account."

- Hugh Mackay

CHAPTER I

The sun was going down on the Carquinez Woods. The few shafts of sunlight that had pierced their pillared gloom were lost in unfathomable depths, or splintered their ineffectual lances on the enormous trunks of the redwoods. For a time the dull red of their vast columns, and the dull red of their cast-off bark which matted the echoless aisles, still seemed to hold a faint glow of the dying day. But even this soon passed. Light and color fled upwards. The dark interlaced treetops, that had all day made an impenetrable shade, broke into fire here and there; their lost spires glittered, faded, and went utterly out. A weird twilight that did not come from the outer world, but seemed born of the wood itself, slowly filled and possessed the aisles. The straight, tall, colossal trunks rose dimly like columns of upward smoke. The few fallen trees stretched their huge length into obscurity, and seemed to lie on shadowy trestles. The strange breath that filled these mysterious vaults had neither coldness nor moisture; a dry, fragrant dust arose from the noiseless foot that trod their bark-strewn floor; the aisles might have been tombs, the fallen trees enormous mummies; the silence the solitude of a forgotten past.

And yet this silence was presently broken by a recurring sound like breathing, interrupted occasionally by inarticulate and stertorous gasps. It was not the quick, panting, listening breath of some stealthy feline or canine animal, but indicated a larger, slower, and more powerful organization, whose progress was less watchful and guarded, or as if a fragment of one of the fallen monsters had become animate. At times this life seemed to take visible form, but as vaguely, as misshapenly, as the phantom of a nightmare. Now it was a square object moving sideways, endways, with neither head nor tail and scarcely visible feet; then an arched bulk rolling against the trunks of the trees and recoiling again, or an upright cylindrical mass, but always oscillating and unsteady, and striking the trees on either hand. The frequent occurrence of the movement suggested the figures of some weird rhythmic dance to music heard by the shape alone. Suddenly it either became motionless or faded away.

There was the frightened neighing of a horse, the sudden jingling of spurs, a shout and outcry, and the swift apparition of three dancing torches in one of the dark aisles; but so intense was the obscurity that they shed no light on surrounding objects, and seemed to advance of their own volition without human guidance, until they disappeared suddenly behind the interposing bulk of one of the largest trees. Beyond its eighty feet of circumference the light could not reach, and the gloom remained inscrutable. But the voices and jingling spurs were heard distinctly.

"Blast the mare! She's shied off that cursed trail again."

"Ye ain't lost it again, hev ye?" growled a second voice.

"That's jist what I hev. And these blasted pine-knots don't give light an inch beyond 'em. D—d if I don't think they make this cursed hole blacker."

There was a laugh—a woman's laugh—hysterical, bitter, sarcastic, exasperating. The second speaker, without heeding it, went on:—

"What in thunder skeert the hosses? Did you see or hear anything?"

"Nothin'. The wood is like a graveyard."

The woman's voice again broke into a hoarse, contemptuous laugh. The man resumed angrily:—

"If you know anything, why in h-ll don't you say so, instead of cackling like a d—d squaw there? P'raps you reckon you ken find the trail too."

"Take this rope off my wrist," said the woman's voice, "untie my hands, let me down, and I'll find it." She spoke quickly and with a Spanish accent.

It was the men's turn to laugh. "And give you a show to snatch that six-shooter and blow a hole through me, as you did to the Sheriff of Calaveras, eh? Not if this court under-stands itself," said the first speaker dryly.

"Go to the devil, then," she said curtly.

"Not before a lady," responded the other. There was another laugh from the men, the spurs jingled again, the three torches reappeared from behind the tree, and then passed away in the darkness.

For a time silence and immutability possessed the woods; the great trunks loomed upwards, their fallen brothers stretched their slow length into obscurity. The sound of breathing again became audible; the shape reappeared in the aisle, and recommenced its mystic dance. Presently it was lost in the shadow of the largest tree, and to the sound of breathing succeeded a grating and scratching of bark. Suddenly, as if riven by lightning, a flash broke from the center of the tree-trunk, lit up the woods, and a sharp report rang through it. After a pause the jingling of spurs and the dancing of torches were revived from the distance.

"Hallo?"

No answer.

"Who fired that shot?"

But there was no reply. A slight veil of smoke passed away to the right, there was the spice of gunpowder in the air, but nothing more.

The torches came forward again, but this time it could be seen they were held in the hands of two men and a woman. The woman's hands were tied at the wrist to the horse-hair reins of her mule, while a riata, passed around her waist and under the mule's girth, was held by one of the men, who were both armed with rifles and revolvers. Their frightened horses curveted, and it was with difficulty they could be made to advance.

"Ho! stranger, what are you shooting at?"

The woman laughed and shrugged her shoulders. "Look yonder at the roots of the tree. You're a d—d smart man for a sheriff, ain't you?"

The man uttered an exclamation and spurred his horse forward, but the animal reared in terror. He then sprang to the ground and approached the tree. The shape lay there, a scarcely distinguishable bulk.

Bret Harte

"A grizzly, by the living Jingo! Shot through the heart."

It was true. The strange shape lit up by the flaring torches seemed more vague, unearthly, and awkward in its dying throes, yet the small shut eyes, the feeble nose, the ponderous shoulders, and half-human foot armed with powerful claws were unmistakable. The men turned by a common impulse and peered into the remote recesses of the wood again.

"Hi, Mister! come and pick up your game. Hallo there!"

The challenge fell unheeded on the empty woods.

"And yet," said he whom the woman had called the sheriff, "he can't be far off. It was a close shot, and the bear hez dropped in his tracks. Why, wot's this sticking in his claws?"

The two men bent over the animal. "Why, it's sugar, brown sugar—look!" There was no mistake. The huge beast's fore paws and muzzle were streaked with the unromantic household provision, and heightened the absurd contrast of its incongruous members. The woman, apparently indifferent, had taken that opportunity to partly free one of her wrists.

"If we hadn't been cavorting round this yer spot for the last half hour, I'd swear there was a shanty not a hundred yards away," said the sheriff.

The other man, without replying, remounted his horse instantly.

"If there is, and it's inhabited by a gentleman that kin make centre shots like that in the dark, and don't care to explain how, I reckon I won't disturb him."

The sheriff was apparently of the same opinion, for he followed his companion's example, and once more led the way. The spurs tinkled, the torches danced, and the cavalcade slowly reentered the gloom. In another moment it had disappeared.

The wood sank again into repose, this time disturbed by neither shape nor sound. What lower forms of life might have crept close to its roots were hidden in the ferns, or passed with deadened tread over the bark-strewn floor. Towards morning a coolness like dew fell from above, with here and there a dropping twig or nut, or the crepitant awakening and stretching-out of cramped and weary branches. Later a dull, lurid dawn, not unlike the last evening's sunset, filled the aisles. This faded again, and a clear gray light, in which every object stood out in sharp distinctness, took its place. Morning was waiting outside in all its brilliant, youthful coloring, but only entered as the matured and sobered day.

Seen in that stronger light, the monstrous tree near which the dead bear lay revealed its age in its denuded and scarred trunk, and showed in its base a deep cavity, a foot or two from the ground, partly hidden by hanging strips of bark which had fallen across it. Suddenly one of these strips was pushed aside, and a young man leaped lightly down.

But for the rifle he carried and some modern peculiarities of dress, he was of a grace so unusual and unconventional that he might have passed for a faun who was quitting his ancestral home. He stepped to the side of the bear with a light elastic movement that was as unlike customary progression as his face and figure were unlike the ordinary types of humanity. Even as he leaned upon his rifle, looking down at the prostrate animal, he unconsciously fell into an attitude that in any other mortal would have been a pose, but with him was the picturesque and unstudied relaxation of perfect symmetry.

"Hallo, Mister!"

He raised his head so carelessly and listlessly that he did not otherwise change his attitude. Stepping from behind the tree, the woman of the preceding night stood before him. Her hands were free except for a thong of the riata, which was still knotted around one wrist, the end of the thong having been torn or burnt away. Her eyes were bloodshot, and her hair hung over her shoulders in one long black braid.

"I reckoned all along it was YOU who shot the bear," she said; "at least some one hiding yer," and she indicated the hollow tree with her hand. "It wasn't no chance shot." Observing that the young man, either from misconception or indifference, did not seem to comprehend her, she added, "We came by here, last night, a minute after you fired."

"Oh, that was YOU kicked up such a row, was it?" said the young man, with a shade of interest.

"I reckon," said the woman, nodding her head, "and them that was with me."

"And who are they?"

"Sheriff Dunn, of Yolo, and his deputy."

"And where are they now?"

"The deputy—in h-ll, I reckon; I don't know about the sheriff."

"I see," said the young man quietly; "and you?"

"I—got away," she said savagely. But she was taken with a sudden nervous shiver, which she at once repressed by tightly dragging her shawl over her shoulders and elbows, and folding her arms defiantly.

"And you're going?"

"To follow the deputy, may be," she said gloomily. "But come, I say, ain't you going to treat? It's cursed cold here."

"Wait a moment." The young man was looking at her, with his arched brows slightly knit and a half smile of curiosity. "Ain't you Teresa?"

She was prepared for the question, but evidently was not certain whether she would reply defiantly or confidently. After an exhaustive scrutiny of his face she chose the latter, and said, "You can bet your life on it, Johnny."

"I don't bet, and my name isn't Johnny. Then you're the woman who stabbed Dick Curson over at Lagrange's?"

She became defiant again.

"That's me, all the time. What are you going to do about it?"

"Nothing. And you used to dance at the Alhambra?" She whisked the shawl from her shoulders, held it up like a scarf, and made one or two steps of the sembicuacua. There was not the least gayety, recklessness, or spontaneity in the action; it was simply mechanical bravado. It was so ineffective, even upon her own feelings, that her arms presently dropped to her side, and she coughed embarrassedly. "Where's that whiskey, pardner?" she asked.

The young man turned toward the tree he had just quitted,

and without further words assisted her to mount to the cavity. It was an irregular-shaped vaulted chamber, pierced fifty feet above by a shaft or cylindrical opening in the decayed trunk, which was blackened by smoke, as if it had served the purpose of a chimney. In one corner lay a bearskin and blanket; at the side were two alcoves or indentations, one of which was evidently used as a table, and the other as a cupboard. In another hollow, near the entrance, lay a few small sacks of flour, coffee, and sugar, the sticky contents of the latter still strewing the floor. From this storehouse the young man drew a wicker flask of whiskey, and handed it, with a tin cup of water, to the woman. She waved the cup aside, placed the flask to her lips, and drank the undiluted spirit. Yet even this was evidently bravado, for the water started to her eyes, and she could not restrain the paroxysm of coughing that followed.

"I reckon that's the kind that kills at forty rods," she said, with a hysterical laugh. "But I say, pardner, you look as if you were fixed here to stay," and she stared ostentatiously around the chamber. But she had already taken in its minutest details, even to observing that the hanging strips of bark could be disposed so as to completely hide the entrance.

"Well, yes," he replied; "it wouldn't be very easy to pull up the stakes and move the shanty further on."

Seeing that either from indifference or caution he had not accepted her meaning, she looked at him fixedly, and said,—

"What is your little game?"

"Eh?"

"What are you hiding for—here, in this tree?"

"But I'm not hiding."

"Then why didn't you come out when they hailed you last night?"

"Because I didn't care to."

Teresa whistled incredulously. "All right—then if you're not hiding, I'm going to." As he did not reply, she went on: "If I can keep out of sight for a couple of weeks, this thing will blow over here, and I can get across into Yolo. I could get a fair show there, where the boys know me. Just now the trails are all watched, but no one would think of lookin' here."

"Then how did you come to think of it?" he asked carelessly.

"Because I knew that bear hadn't gone far for that sugar; because I know he hadn't stole it from a cache—it was too fresh, and we'd have seen the torn-up earth; because we had passed no camp; and because I knew there was no shanty here. And, besides," she added in a low voice, "maybe I was huntin' a hole myself to die in—and spotted it by instinct."

There was something in this suggestion of a hunted animal that, unlike anything she had previously said or suggested, was not exaggerated, and caused the young man to look at her again. She was standing under the chimney-like opening, and the light from above illuminated her head and shoulders. The pupils of her eyes had lost their feverish prominence, and were slightly suffused and softened as she gazed abstractedly before her. The only vestige of her previous excitement was in her left-hand fingers, which were incessantly twisting and turning a diamond ring upon her right hand, but without imparting the least animation to her rigid attitude. Suddenly, as if conscious of his scrutiny, she stepped aside out of the revealing light and by a swift feminine instinct raised her hand to her head as if to adjust her straggling hair. It was only for a moment, however, for, as if aware of the weakness, she struggled to resume her aggressive pose.

"Well," she said. "Speak up. Am I goin' to stop here, or have I got to get up and get?"

"You can stay," said the young man quietly; "but as I've got my provisions and ammunition here, and haven't any other place to go to just now, I suppose we'll have to share it together."

She glanced at him under her eyelids, and a half-bitter, half-contemptuous smile passed across her face. "All right, old man," she said, holding out her hand, "it's a go. We'll start in housekeeping at once, if you like."

"I'll have to come here once or twice a day," he said, quite composedly, "to look after my things, and get something to eat; but I'll be away most of the time, and what with camping out under the trees every night I reckon my share won't incommode you."

She opened her black eyes upon him, at this original proposition. Then she looked down at her torn dress. "I suppose this style of thing ain't very fancy, is it?" she said, with a forced laugh.

"I think I know where to beg or borrow a change for you, if you can't get any," he replied simply.

She stared at him again. "Are you a family man?"

"No."

She was silent for a moment. "Well," she said, "you can tell your girl I'm not particular about its being in the latest fashion."

There was a slight flush on his forehead as he turned toward the little cupboard, but no tremor in his voice as he went on: "You'll find tea and coffee here, and, if you're bored, there's a book or two. You read, don't you—I mean English?"

She nodded, but cast a look of undisguised contempt upon the two worn, coverless novels he held out to her. "You haven't got last week's 'Sacramento Union,' have you? I hear they have my case all in; only them lying reporters made it out against me all the time."

"I don't see the papers," he replied curtly.

"They say there's a picture of me in the 'Police Gazette,' taken in the act," and she laughed.

He looked a little abstracted, and turned as if to go. "I think you'll do well to rest a while just now, and keep as close hid as possible until afternoon. The trail is a mile away at the nearest point, but some one might miss it and stray over here. You're quite safe if you're careful, and stand by the tree. You can build a fire here," he stepped under the chimney-like opening, "without its being noticed. Even the smoke is lost and cannot be seen so high."

The light from above was falling on his head and shoulders, as it had on hers. She looked at him intently.

"You travel a good deal on your figure, pardner, don't you?" she said, with a certain admiration that was quite sexless in its quality; "but I don't see how you pick up a living by it in the Carquinez Woods. So you're going, are you? You might be more sociable. Good-by."

"Good-by!" He leaped from the opening.

"I say pardner!"

He turned a little impatiently. She had knelt down at the entrance, so as to be nearer his level, and was holding out her hand. But he did not notice it, and she quietly withdrew it.

"If anybody dropped in and asked for you, what name will they say?"

He smiled. "Don't wait to hear."

"But suppose I wanted to sing out for you, what will I call you?"

He hesitated. "Call me—Lo."

"Lo, the poor Indian?"*

"Exactly."

> * The first word of Pope's familiar apostrophe is humorously used in the Far West as a distinguishing title for the Indian.

It suddenly occurred to the woman, Teresa, that in the young man's height, supple, yet erect carriage, color, and singular gravity of demeanor there was a refined, aboriginal suggestion. He did not look like any Indian she had ever seen, but rather as a youthful chief might have looked. There was a further suggestion in his fringed buckskin shirt and moccasins; but before she could utter the half-sarcastic comment that rose to her lips he had glided noiselessly away, even as an Indian might have done.

She readjusted the slips of hanging bark with feminine ingenuity, dispersing them so as to completely hide the entrance. Yet this did not darken the chamber, which seemed to draw a purer and more vigorous light through the soaring shaft that pierced the roof than that which came from the dim woodland aisles below. Nevertheless, she shivered, and drawing her shawl closely around her began to collect some half-burnt fragments of wood in the chimney to make a fire. But the preoccupation of her thoughts rendered this a tedious process, as she would from time to time stop in the middle of an action and fall into an attitude of rapt abstraction, with far-off eyes and rigid mouth. When she had at last succeeded in kindling a fire and raising a film of pale blue smoke, that seemed to fade and dissipate entirely before it reached the top of the chimney shaft, she crouched beside it, fixed her eyes on the darkest corner of the cavern, and became motionless.

What did she see through that shadow?

Nothing at first but a confused medley of figures and incidents of the preceding night; things to be put away and forgotten; things that would not have happened but for another thing—the thing before which everything faded! A ball-room; the sounds of music; the one man she had cared for insulting her with the flaunting ostentation of his unfaithfulness; herself despised, put aside, laughed at, or worse, jilted. And then the moment of delirium, when the light danced; the one wild act that lifted her, the despised one, above them all—made her the supreme figure, to be glanced at by frightened women, stared at by half-startled, half-admiring men! "Yes," she laughed; but struck by the sound of her own voice, moved twice round the cavern nervously, and then dropped again into her old position.

As they carried him away he had laughed at her—like a hound that he was; he who had praised her for her spirit, and incited her revenge against others; he who had taught her to strike when she was insulted; and it was only fit he should reap what he had sown. She was what he, what other men, had made her. And what was she now? What had she been once?

She tried to recall her childhood: the man and woman who might have been her father and mother; who fought and wrangled over her precocious little life; abused or caressed her as she sided with either; and then left her with a circus troupe, where she first tasted the power of her courage, her beauty, and her recklessness. She remembered those flashes of triumph that left a fever in her veins—a fever that when it failed must be stimulated by dissipation, by anything, by everything that would keep her name a wonder in men's mouths, an envious fear to women. She recalled her transfer to the strolling players; her cheap pleasures, and cheaper rivalries and hatred—but always Teresa! the daring Teresa! the reckless Teresa! audacious as a woman, invincible as a boy; dancing, flirting, fencing, shooting, swearing, drinking, smoking, fighting Teresa! "Oh, yes; she had been loved, perhaps—who knows?—but always feared. Why should she change now? Ha, he should see."

She had lashed herself in a frenzy, as was her wont, with gestures, ejaculations, oaths, adjurations, and passionate apostrophes, but with this strange and unexpected result. Heretofore she had always been sustained and kept up by an audience of some kind or quality, if only perhaps a humble companion; there had always been some one she could fascinate or horrify, and she could read her power mirrored in their eyes. Even the half-abstracted indifference of her strange host had been something. But she was alone now. Her words fell on apathetic solitude; she was acting to viewless space. She rushed to the opening, dashed the hanging bark aside, and leaped to the ground.

She ran forward wildly a few steps, and stopped.

"Hallo!" she cried. "Look, 'tis I, Teresa!"

The profound silence remained unbroken. Her shrillest tones were lost in an echoless space, even as the smoke of her fire had faded into pure ether. She stretched out her clenched fists as if to defy the pillared austerities of the vaults around her.

"Come and take me if you dare!"

The challenge was unheeded. If she had thrown herself violently against the nearest tree-trunk, she could not have been stricken more breathless than she was by the compact, embattled solitude that encompassed her. The hopelessness of impressing these cold and passive vaults with her selfish passion filled her with a vague fear. In her rage of the previous night she had not seen the wood in its profound immobility. Left alone with the majesty of those enormous columns, she trembled and turned faint. The silence of the hollow tree she had just quitted seemed to her less awful than the crushing presence of these mute and monstrous witnesses of her weakness. Like a wounded quail with lowered crest and trailing wing, she crept back to her hiding place.

Even then the influence of the wood was still upon her. She picked up the novel she had contemptuously thrown aside, only to let it fall again in utter weariness. For a moment her feminine curiosity was excited by the discovery of an old book, in whose blank leaves were pressed a variety of flowers and woodland grasses. As she could not conceive that these had been kept for any but a sentimental purpose, she was disappointed to find that underneath each was a sentence in an unknown tongue, that even to her untutored eye did not appear to be the language of passion. Finally she rearranged the couch of skins and blankets, and, imparting to it in three clever shakes an entirely different character, lay down to pursue her reveries. But nature asserted herself, and ere she knew it she was asleep.

So intense and prolonged had been her previous excitement that, the tension once relieved, she passed into a slumber of exhaustion so deep that she seemed scarce to breathe. High noon succeeded morning, the central shaft received a single ray of upper sunlight, the afternoon came and went, the shadows gathered below, the sunset fires began to eat their way through the groined roof, and she still slept. She slept even when the bark hangings of the chamber were put aside, and the young man reentered.

He laid down a bundle he was carrying and softly approached the sleeper. For a moment he was startled from his indifference; she lay so still and motionless. But this was not all that struck him; the face before him was no longer the passionate, haggard visage that confronted him that morning; the feverish air, the burning color, the strained muscles of mouth and brow, and the staring eyes were gone; wiped away, perhaps, by the tears that still left their traces on cheek and dark eyelash. It was the face of a handsome woman of thirty, with even a suggestion of softness in the contour of the cheek and arching of her upper lip, no longer rigidly drawn down in anger, but relaxed by sleep on her white teeth.

With the lithe, soft tread that was habitual to him, the young man moved about, examining the condition of the little chamber and its stock of provisions and necessaries, and withdrew presently, to reappear as noiselessly with a tin bucket of water. This done, he replenished the little pile of fuel with an armful of bark and pine cones, cast an approving glance about him, which included the sleeper, and silently departed.

It was night when she awoke. She was surrounded by a profound darkness, except where the shaft-like opening made a nebulous mist in the corner of her wooden cavern. Providentially she struggled back to consciousness slowly, so that the solitude and silence came upon her gradually, with a growing realization of the events of the past twenty-four hours, but without a shock. She was alone here, but safe still, and every hour added to her chances of ultimate escape. She remembered to have seen a candle among the articles on the shelf, and she began to grope her way towards the matches. Suddenly she stopped. What was that panting?

Was it her own breathing, quickened with a sudden nameless terror? or was there something outside? Her heart seemed to stop beating while she listened. Yes! it was a panting outside—a panting now increased, multiplied, redoubled, mixed with the sounds of rustling, tearing, craunching, and occasionally a quick, impatient snarl. She crept on her hands and knees to the opening and looked out. At first the ground seemed to be undulating between her and the opposite tree. But a second glance showed her the black and gray, bristling, tossing backs of tumbling beasts of prey, charging the carcass of the bear that lay at its roots, or contesting for the prize with gluttonous, choked breath, sidelong snarls, arched spines, and recurved tails. One of the boldest had leaped upon a buttressing root of her tree within a foot of the opening. The excitement, awe, and terror she had undergone culminated in one wild, maddened scream, that seemed to pierce even the cold depths of the forest, as she dropped on her face, with her hands clasped over her eyes in an agony of fear.

Her scream was answered, after a pause, by a sudden volley of firebrands and sparks into the midst of the panting, crowding pack; a few smothered howls and snaps, and a sudden dispersion of the concourse. In another moment the young man, with a blazing brand in either hand, leaped upon the body of the bear.

Teresa raised her head, uttered a hysterical cry, slid down the tree, flew wildly to his side, caught convulsively at his sleeve, and fell on her knees beside him.

"Save me! save me!" she gasped, in a voice broken by terror. "Save me from those hideous creatures. No, no!" she implored, as he endeavored to lift her to her feet. "No—let me stay here close beside you. So," clutching the fringe of his leather hunting-shirt, and dragging herself on her knees nearer him—"so—don't leave me, for God's sake!"

"They are gone," he replied, gazing down curiously at her, as she wound the fringe around her hand to strengthen her hold; "they're only a lot of cowardly coyotes and wolves, that dare not attack anything that lives and can move."

The young woman responded with a nervous shudder. "Yes, that's it," she whispered, in a broken voice; "it's only the dead they want. Promise me—swear to me, if I'm caught, or hung, or shot, you won't let me be left here to be torn and—ah! my God! what's that?"

She had thrown her arms around his knees, completely pinioning him to her frantic breast. Something like a smile of disdain passed across his face as he answered, "It's nothing. They will not return. Get up!"

Even in her terror she saw the change in his face. "I know, I know!" she cried. "I'm frightened—but I cannot bear it any longer. Hear me! Listen! Listen—but don't move! I didn't mean to kill Curson—no! I swear to God, no! I didn't mean to kill the sheriff—and I didn't. I was only bragging—do you hear? I lied! I lied—don't move, I swear to God I lied. I've made myself out worse than I was. I have. Only don't leave me now—and if I die—and it's not far off, may be—get me away from here—and from THEM. Swear it!"

"All right," said the young man, with a scarcely concealed movement of irritation. "But get up now, and go back to the cabin."

"No; not THERE alone." Nevertheless, he quietly but firmly released himself.

"I will stay here," he replied. "I would have been nearer to you, but I thought it better for your safety that my camp-fire should be further off. But I can build it here, and that will keep the coyotes off."

"Let me stay with you—beside you," she said imploringly.

She looked so broken, crushed, and spiritless, so unlike the woman of the morning that, albeit with an ill grace, he tacitly consented, and turned away to bring his blankets. But in the next moment she was at his side, following him like a dog, silent and wistful, and even offering to carry his burden. When he had built the fire, for which she had collected the pine-cones and broken branches near them, he sat down, folded his arms, and leaned back against the tree in reserved and deliberate silence.

Humble and submissive, she did not attempt to break in upon a reverie she could not help but feel had little kindliness to herself. As the fire snapped and sparkled, she pillowed her head upon a root, and lay still to watch it.

It rose and fell, and dying away at times to a mere lurid glow, and again, agitated by some breath scarcely perceptible to them, quickening into a roaring flame. When only the embers remained, a dead silence filled the wood. Then the first breath of morning moved the tangled canopy above, and a dozen tiny sprays and needles detached from the interlocked boughs winged their soft way noiselessly to the earth. A few fell upon the prostrate woman like a gentle benediction, and she slept. But even then, the young man, looking down, saw that the slender fingers were still aimlessly but rigidly twisted in the leather fringe of his hunting-shirt.

CHAPTER II

It was a peculiarity of the Carquinez Wood that it stood apart and distinct in its gigantic individuality. Even where the integrity of its own singular species was not entirely preserved, it admitted no inferior trees. Nor was there any diminishing fringe on its outskirts; the sentinels that guarded the few gateways of the dim trails were as monstrous as the serried ranks drawn up in the heart of the forest. Consequently, the red highway that skirted the eastern angle was bare and shadeless, until it slipped a league off into a watered valley and refreshed itself under lesser sycamores and willows. It was here the newly born city of Excelsior, still in its cradle, had, like an infant Hercules, strangled the serpentine North Fork of the American river, and turned its life current into the ditches and flumes of the Excelsior mines.

Newest of the new houses that seemed to have accidentally formed its single, straggling street was the residence of the Rev. Winslow Wynn, not unfrequently known as "Father Wynn," pastor of the First Baptist church. The "pastorage," as it was cheerfully called, had the glaring distinction of being built of brick, and was, as had been wickedly pointed out by idle scoffers, the only "fireproof" structure in town. This sarcasm was not, however, supposed to be particularly distasteful to "Father Wynn," who enjoyed the reputation of being "hail fellow, well met" with the rough mining element, who called them by their Christian names, had been known to drink at the bar of the Polka Saloon while engaged in the conversion of a prominent citizen, and was popularly said to have no "gospel starch" about him. Certain conscious outcasts and transgressors were touched at this apparent unbending of the spiritual authority. The rigid tenets of Father Wynn's faith were lost in the supposed catholicity of his humanity. "A preacher that can jine a man when he's histin' liquor into him, without jawin' about it, ought to be allowed to wrestle with sinners and splash about in as much cold water as he likes," was the criticism of one of his converts. Nevertheless, it was true that Father Wynn was somewhat loud and intolerant in his tolerance. It was true that he was a little more rough, a little more frank, a little more hearty, a little more impulsive than his disciples. It was true that often the proclamation of his extreme liberality and brotherly equality partook somewhat of an apology. It is true that a few who might have been most benefited by this kind of gospel regarded him with a singular disdain. It is true that his liberality was of an ornamental, insinuating quality, accompanied with but little sacrifice; his acceptance of a collection taken up in a gambling saloon for the rebuilding of his church, destroyed by fire, gave him a popularity large enough, it must be confessed, to cover the sins of the gamblers themselves, but it was not proven that HE had ever organized any form of relief. But it was true that local history somehow accepted him as an exponent of mining Christianity, without the least reference to the opinions of the Christian miners themselves.

The Rev. Mr. Wynn's liberal habits and opinions were not, however, shared by his only daughter, a motherless young lady of eighteen. Nellie Wynn was in the eye of Excelsior an unapproachable divinity, as inaccessible and cold as her father was impulsive and familiar. An atmosphere of chaste and proud virginity made itself felt even in the starched integrity of her spotless skirts, in her neatly gloved finger-tips, in her clear amber eyes, in her imperious red lips, in her sensitive nostrils. Need it be said that the youth and middle age of Excelsior were madly, because apparently hopelessly, in love with her? For the rest, she had been expensively educated, was profoundly ignorant in two languages, with a trained misunderstanding of music and painting, and a natural and faultless taste in dress.

The Rev. Mr. Wynn was engaged in a characteristic hearty parting with one of his latest converts, upon his own doorstep, with admirable al fresco effect. He had just clapped him on the shoulder. "Good-by, good-by, Charley, my boy, and keep in the right path; not up, or down, or round the gulch, you know—ha, ha!—but straight across lots to the shining gate." He had raised his voice under the stimulus of a few admiring spectators, and backed his convert playfully against the wall. "You see! we're goin' in to win, you bet. Good-by! I'd ask you to step in and have a chat, but I've got my work to do, and so have you. The gospel mustn't keep us from that, must it, Charley? Ha, ha!"

The convert (who elsewhere was a profane expressman, and had become quite imbecile under Mr. Wynn's active hearti-ness and brotherly horse-play before spectators) managed, however, to feebly stammer with a blush something about "Miss Nellie."

"Ah, Nellie. She, too, is at her tasks—trimming her lamp—you know, the parable of the wise virgins," continued Father Wynn hastily, fearing that the convert might take the illustration literally. "There, there—good-by. Keep in the right path." And with a parting shove he dismissed Charley and entered his own house.

That "wise virgin," Nellie, had evidently finished with the lamp, and was now going out to meet the bridegroom, as she was fully dressed and gloved, and had a pink parasol in her hand, as her father entered the sitting-room. His bluff heartiness seemed to fade away as he removed his soft, broad-brimmed hat and glanced across the too fresh-looking apartment. There was a smell of mortar still in the air, and a faint suggestion that at any moment green grass might appear between the interstices of the red-brick hearth. The room, yielding a little in the point of coldness, seemed to share Miss Nellie's fresh virginity, and, barring the pink parasol, set her off as in a vestal's cell.

"I supposed you wouldn't care to see Brace, the expressman, so I got rid of him at the door," said her father, drawing one of the new chairs towards him slowly, and sitting down carefully, as if it were a hitherto untried experiment.

Miss Nellie's face took a tint of interest. "Then he doesn't go with the coach to Indian Spring to-day?"

"No; why?"

"I thought of going over myself to get the Burnham girls to come to choir-meeting," replied Miss Nellie carelessly, "and he might have been company."

"He'd go now, if he knew you were going," said her father; "but it's just as well he shouldn't be needlessly encouraged. I rather think that Sheriff Dunn is a little jealous of him. By the way, the sheriff is much better. I called to cheer him up to-day" (Mr. Wynn had in fact tumultuously accelerated the sick man's pulse), "and he talked of you, as usual. In fact, he said he had only two things to get well for. One was to catch and hang that woman Teresa, who shot him; the other—can't you guess the other?" he added archly, with a faint suggestion of his other manner.

Miss Nellie coldly could not.

The Rev. Mr. Wynn's archness vanished. "Don't be a fool," he said dryly. "He wants to marry you, and you know it."

"Most of the men here do," responded Miss Nellie, without the least trace of coquetry. "Is the wedding or the hanging to take place first, or together, so he can officiate at both?"

"His share in the Union Ditch is worth a hundred thousand dollars," continued her father; "and if he isn't nominated for district judge this fall, he's bound to go to the legislature, anyway. I don't think a girl with your advantages and education can afford to throw away the chance of shining in Sacramento, San Francisco, or, in good time, perhaps even Washington."

Miss Nellie's eyes did not reflect entire disapproval of this suggestion, although she replied with something of her father's practical quality.

"Mr. Dunn is not out of his bed yet, and they say Teresa's got away to Arizona, so there isn't any particular hurry."

"Perhaps not; but see here, Nellie, I've some important news for you. You know your young friend of the Carquinez Woods—Dorman, the botanist, eh? Well, Brace knows all about him. And what do you think he is?"

Miss Nellie took upon herself a few extra degrees of cold, and didn't know.

"An Injin! Yes, an out-and-out Cherokee. You see he calls himself Dorman—Low Dorman. That's only French for

'Sleeping Water,' his Injin name!—'Low Dorman.'"

"You mean 'L'Eau Dormante,'" said Nellie.

"That's what I said. The chief called him 'Sleeping Water' when he was a boy, and one of them French Canadian trappers translated it into French when he brought him to California to school. But he's an Injin, sure. No wonder he prefers to live in the woods."

"Well?" said Nellie.

"Well," echoed her father impatiently, "he's an Injin, I tell you, and you can't of course have anything to do with him. He mustn't come here again."

"But you forget," said Nellie imperturbably, "that it was you who invited him here, and were so much exercised over him. You remember you introduced him to the Bishop and those Eastern clergymen as a magnificent specimen of a young Californian. You forget what an occasion you made of his coming to church on Sunday, and how you made him come in his buckskin shirt and walk down the street with you after service!"

"Yes, yes," said the Rev. Mr. Wynn, hurriedly.

"And," continued Nellie carelessly, "how you made us sing out of the same book 'Children of our Father's Fold,' and how you preached at him until he actually got a color!"

"Yes," said her father; "but it wasn't known then he was an Injin, and they are frightfully unpopular with those South-western men among whom we labor. Indeed, I am quite convinced that when Brace said 'the only good Indian was a dead one' his expression, though extravagant, perhaps, really voiced the sentiments of the majority. It would be only kindness to the unfortunate creature to warn him from exposing himself to their rude but conscientious antagonism."

"Perhaps you'd better tell him, then, in your own popular way, which they all seem to understand so well," responded the daughter. Mr. Wynn cast a quick glance at her, but there was no trace of irony in her face—nothing but a half-bored indifference as she walked toward the window.

"I will go with you to the coach-office," said her father, who generally gave these simple paternal duties the pronounced character of a public Christian example.

"It's hardly worth while," replied Miss Nellie. "I've to stop at the Watsons', at the foot of the hill, and ask after the baby; so I shall go on to the Crossing and pick up the coach when it passes. Good-by."

Nevertheless, as soon as Nellie had departed, the Rev. Mr. Wynn proceeded to the coach-office, and publicly grasping the hand of Yuba Bill, the driver, commended his daughter to his care in the name of the universal brotherhood of man and the Christian fraternity. Carried away by his heartiness, he forgot his previous caution, and confided to the express-man Miss Nellie's regrets that she was not to have that gentleman's company. The result was that Miss Nellie found the coach with its passengers awaiting her with uplifted hats and wreathed smiles at the Crossing, and the box seat (from which an unfortunate stranger, who had expensively paid for it, had been summarily ejected) at her service beside Yuba Bill, who had thrown away his cigar and donned a new pair of buckskin gloves to do her honor. But a more serious result to the young beauty was the effect of the Rev. Mr. Wynn's confidences upon the impulsive heart of Jack Brace, the expressman. It has been already intimated that it was his "day off." Unable to summarily reassume his usual functions beside the driver without some practical reason, and ashamed to go so palpably as a mere passenger, he was forced to let the coach proceed without him. Discomfited for the moment, he was not, however, beaten. He had lost the blissful journey by her side, which would have been his professional right, but—she was going to Indian Spring! could he not anticipate her there? Might they not meet in the most accidental manner? And what might not come from that meeting away from the prying eyes of their own town? Mr. Brace did not hesitate, but saddling his fleet Buckskin, by the time the stage-coach had passed the Crossing in the high-road he had mounted the hill and was dashing along the "cutoff" in the same direction, a full mile in advance. Arriving at Indian Spring, he left his horse at a Mexican posada on the confines of the settlement, and from the piled debris of a tunnel excavation awaited the slow arrival of the coach. On mature reflection he could give no reason why he had not boldly awaited it at the express office, except a certain bashful consciousness of his own folly, and a belief that it might be glaringly apparent to the bystanders. When the coach arrived and he had overcome this consciousness, it was too late. Yuba Bill had discharged his passengers for Indian Spring and driven away. Miss Nellie was in the settlement, but where? As time passed he became more desperate and bolder. He walked recklessly up and down the main street, glancing in at the open doors of shops, and even in the windows of private dwellings. It might have seemed a poor compliment to Miss Nellie, but it was an evidence of his complete preoccupation, when the sight of a female face at a window, even though it was plain or perhaps painted, caused his heart to bound, or the glancing of a skirt in the distance quickened his feet and his pulses. Had Jack contented himself with remaining at Excelsior he might have vaguely regretted, but as soon become as vaguely accustomed to, Miss Nellie's absence. But it was not until his hitherto quiet and passive love took this first step of action that it fully declared itself. When he had made the tour of the town a dozen times unsuccessfully, he had perfectly made up his mind that marriage with Nellie or the speedy death of several people, including possibly himself, was the only alternative. He regretted he had not accompanied her; he regretted he had not demanded where she was going; he contemplated a course of future action that two hours ago would have filled him with bashful terror. There was clearly but one thing to do—to declare his passion the instant he met her, and return with her to Excelsior an accepted suitor, or not to return at all.

Suddenly he was vexatiously conscious of hearing his name lazily called, and looking up found that he was on the outskirts of the town, and interrogated by two horsemen.

"Got down to walk, and the coach got away from you, Jack, eh?"

A little ashamed of his preoccupation, Brace stammered something about "collections." He did not recognize the men, but his own face, name, and business were familiar to everybody for fifty miles along the stage-road.

"Well, you can settle a bet for us, I reckon. Bill Dacre thar bet me five dollars and the drinks that a young gal we met at the edge of the Carquinez Woods, dressed in a long brown duster and half muffled up in a hood, was the daughter of Father Wynn of Excelsior. I did not get a fair look at her, but it stands to reason that a high-toned young lady like Nellie Wynn don't go trap'sing along the wood like a Pike County tramp. I took the bet. May be you know if she's here or in Excelsior?"

Mr. Brace felt himself turning pale with eagerness and

excitement. But the near prospect of seeing her presently gave him back his caution, and he answered truthfully that he had left her in Excelsior, and that in his two hours' sojourn in Indian Spring he had not met her once. "But," he added, with a Californian's reverence for the sanctity of a bet, "I reckon you'd better make it a stand-off for twenty-four hours, and I'll find out and let you know." Which, it is only fair to say, he honestly intended to do.

With a hurried nod of parting, he continued in the direction of the Woods. When he had satisfied himself that the strangers had entered the settlement, and would not follow him for further explanation, he quickened his pace. In half an hour he passed between two of the gigantic sentinels that guarded the entrance to a trail. Here he paused to collect his thoughts. The Woods were vast in extent, the trail dim and uncertain—at times apparently breaking off, or intersecting another trail as faint as itself. Believing that Miss Nellie had diverged from the highway only as a momentary excursion into the shade, and that she would not dare to penetrate its more sombre and unknown recesses, he kept within sight of the skirting plain. By degrees the sedate influence of the silent vaults seemed to depress him. The ardor of the chase began to flag. Under the calm of their dim roof the fever of his veins began to subside; his pace slackened; he reasoned more deliberately. It was by no means probable that the young woman in a brown duster was Nellie; it was not her habitual traveling dress; it was not like her to walk unattended in the road; there was nothing in her tastes and habits to take her into this gloomy forest, allowing that she had even entered it; and on this absolute question of her identity the two witnesses were divided. He stopped irresolutely, and cast a last, long, half-despairing look around him. Hitherto he had given that part of the wood nearest the plain his greatest attention. His glance now sought its darker recesses. Suddenly he became breathless. Was it a beam of sunlight that had pierced the groined roof above, and now rested against the trunk of one of the dimmer, more secluded giants? No, it was moving; even as he gazed it slipped away, glanced against another tree, passed across one of the vaulted aisles, and then was lost again. Brief as was the glimpse, he was not mistaken—it was the figure of a woman.

In another moment he was on her track, and soon had the satisfaction of seeing her reappear at a lesser distance. But the continual intervention of the massive trunks made the chase by no means an easy one, and as he could not keep her always in sight he was unable to follow or understand the one intelligent direction which she seemed to invariably keep. Nevertheless, he gained upon her breathlessly, and, thanks to the bark-strewn floor, noiselessly. He was near enough to distinguish and recognize the dress she wore, a pale yellow, that he had admired when he first saw her. It was Nellie, unmistakably; if it were she of the brown duster, she had discarded it, perhaps for greater freedom. He was near enough to call out now, but a sudden nervous timidity overcame him; his lips grew dry. What should he say to her? How account for his presence? "Miss Nellie, one moment!" he gasped. She darted forward and—vanished.

At this moment he was not more than a dozen yards from her. He rushed to where she had been standing, but her disappearance was perfect and complete. He made a circuit of the group of trees within whose radius she had last appeared, but there was neither trace of her, nor a suggestion of her mode of escape. He called aloud to her; the vacant Woods let his helpless voice die in their unresponsive depths. He gazed into the air and down at the bark-strewn carpet at his feet. Like most of his vocation, he was sparing of speech, and epigrammatic after his fashion. Compre-hending in one swift but despairing flash of intelligence the existence of some fateful power beyond his own weak

Bret Harte

endeavor, he accepted its logical result with characteristic grimness, threw his hat upon the ground, put his hands in his pockets, and said—

"Well, I'm d—d!"

CHAPTER III

Out of compliment to Miss Nellie Wynn, Yuba Bill, on reaching Indian Spring, had made a slight detour to enable him to ostentatiously set down his fair passenger before the door of the Burnhams. When it had closed on the admiring eyes of the passengers and the coach had rattled away, Miss Nellie, without any undue haste or apparent change in her usual quiet demeanor, managed, however, to dispatch her business promptly, and, leaving an impression that she would call again before her return to Excelsior, parted from her friends and slipped away through a side street to the General Furnishing Store of Indian Spring. In passing this emporium, Miss Nellie's quick eye had discovered a cheap brown linen duster hanging in its window. To purchase it, and put it over her delicate cambric dress, albeit with a shivering sense that she looked like a badly folded brown-paper parcel, did not take long. As she left the shop it was with mixed emotions of chagrin and security that she noticed that her passage through the settlement no longer turned the heads of its male inhabitants. She reached the outskirts of Indian Spring and the high-road at about the time Mr. Brace had begun his fruitless patrol of the main street. Far in the distance a faint olive-green table mountain seemed to rise abruptly from the plain. It was the Carquinez Woods. Gathering her spotless skirts beneath her extemporized brown domino, she set out briskly towards them.

Bret Harte

But her progress was scarcely free or exhilarating. She was not accustomed to walking in a country where "buggy-riding" was considered the only genteel young-lady-like mode of progression, and its regular provision the expected courtesy of mankind. Always fastidiously booted, her low-quartered shoes were charming to the eye, but hardly adapted to the dust and inequalities of the highroad. It was true that she had thought of buying a coarser pair at Indian Spring, but once face to face with their uncompromising ugliness, she had faltered and fled. The sun was unmistakably hot, but her parasol was too well known and offered too violent a contrast to the duster for practical use. Once she stopped with an exclamation of annoyance, hesitated, and looked back. In half an hour she had twice lost her shoe and her temper; a pink flush took possession of her cheeks, and her eyes were bright with suppressed rage. Dust began to form grimy circles around their orbits; with cat-like shivers she even felt it pervade the roots of her blond hair. Gradually her breath grew more rapid and hysterical, her smarting eyes became humid, and at last, encountering two observant horsemen in the road, she turned and fled, until, reaching the wood, she began to cry.

Nevertheless she waited for the two horsemen to pass, to satisfy herself that she was not followed; then pushed on vaguely, until she reached a fallen tree, where, with a gesture of disgust, she tore off her hapless duster and flung it on the ground. She then sat down sobbing, but after a moment dried her eyes hurriedly and started to her feet. A few paces distant, erect, noiseless, with outstretched hand, the young solitary of the Carquinez Woods advanced towards her. His hand had almost touched hers, when he stopped.

"What has happened?" he asked gravely.

"Nothing," she said, turning half away, and searching the

ground with her eyes, as if she had lost something. "Only I must be going back now."

"You shall go back at once, if you wish it," he said, flushing slightly. "But you have been crying; why?"

Frank as Miss Nellie wished to be, she could not bring herself to say that her feet hurt her, and the dust and heat were ruining her complexion. It was therefore with a half-confident belief that her troubles were really of a moral quality that she answered, "Nothing—nothing, but—but—it's wrong to come here."

"But you did not think it was wrong when you agreed to come, at our last meeting," said the young man, with that persistent logic which exasperates the inconsequent feminine mind. "It cannot be any more wrong to-day."

"But it was not so far off," murmured the young girl, without looking up.

"Oh, the distance makes it more improper, then," he said abstractedly; but after a moment's contemplation of her half-averted face, he asked gravely, "Has anyone talked to you about me?"

Ten minutes before, Nellie had been burning to unburthen herself of her father's warning, but now she felt she would not. "I wish you wouldn't call yourself Low," she said at last.

"But it's my name," he replied quietly.

"Nonsense! It's only a stupid translation of a stupid nickname. They might as well call you 'Water' at once."

"But you said you liked it."

"Well, so I do. But don't you see—I—oh dear! you don't understand."

Low did not reply, but turned his head with resigned gravity towards the deeper woods. Grasping the barrel of his rifle with his left hand, he threw his right arm across his left wrist and leaned slightly upon it with the habitual ease of a Western hunter—doubly picturesque in his own lithe, youthful symmetry. Miss Nellie looked at him from under her eyelids, and then half defiantly raised her head and her dark lashes. Gradually an almost magical change came over her features; her eyes grew larger and more and more yearning, until they seemed to draw and absorb in their liquid depths the figure of the young man before her; her cold face broke into an ecstasy of light and color; her humid lips parted in a bright, welcoming smile, until, with an irresistible impulse, she arose, and throwing back her head stretched towards him two hands full of vague and trembling passion.

In another moment he had seized them, kissed them, and, as he drew her closer to his embrace, felt them tighten around his neck. "But what name do you wish to call me?" he asked, looking down into her eyes.

Miss Nellie murmured something confidentially to the third button of his hunting shirt. "But that," he replied, with a smile, "THAT wouldn't be any more practical, and you wouldn't want others to call me dar—" Her fingers loosened around his neck, she drew her head back, and a singular expression passed over her face, which to any calmer observer than a lover would have seemed, however, to indicate more curiosity than jealousy.

"Who else DOES call you so?" she added earnestly. "How many, for instance?"

Low's reply was addressed not to her ear, but her lips. She did not avoid it, but added, "And do you kiss them all like that?" Taking him by the shoulders, she held him a little way from her, and gazed at him from head to foot. Then drawing him again to her embrace, she said, "I don't care, at least no woman has kissed you like that." Happy, dazzled, and embarrassed, he was beginning to stammer the truthful protestation that rose to his lips, but she stopped him: "No, don't protest! say nothing! Let ME love YOU—that is all. It is enough." He would have caught her in his arms again, but she drew back. "We are near the road," she said quietly. "Come! You promised to show me where you camped. Let US make the most of our holiday. In an hour I must leave the woods."

"But I shall accompany you, dearest."

"No, I must go as I came—alone."

"But Nellie—"

"I tell you no," she said, with an almost harsh practical decision, incompatible with her previous abandonment. "We might be seen together."

"Well, suppose we are; we must be seen together eventually," he remonstrated.

The young girl made an involuntary gesture of impatient negation, but checked herself. "Don't let us talk of that now. Come, while I am here under your own roof—" she pointed to the high interlaced boughs above them—"you must be hospitable. Show me your home; tell me, isn't it a little gloomy sometimes?"

"It never has been; I never thought it WOULD be until the

moment you leave it to-day."

She pressed his hand briefly and in a half-perfunctory way, as if her vanity had accepted and dismissed the compliment. "Take me somewhere," she said inquisitively, "where you stay most; I do not seem to see you HERE," she added, looking around her with a slight shiver. "It is so big and so high. Have you no place where you eat and rest and sleep?"

"Except in the rainy season, I camp all over the place—at any spot where I may have been shooting or collecting."

"Collecting?" queried Nellie.

"Yes; with the herbarium, you know."

"Yes," said Nellie dubiously. "But you told me once—the first time we ever talked together," she added, looking in his eyes—"something about your keeping your things like a squirrel in a tree. Could we not go there? Is there not room for us to sit and talk without being brow-beaten and looked down upon by these supercilious trees?"

"It's too far away," said Low truthfully, but with a somewhat pronounced emphasis, "much too far for you just now; and it lies on another trail that enters the wood beyond. But come, I will show you a spring known only to myself, the wood ducks, and the squirrels. I discovered it the first day I saw you, and gave it your name. But you shall christen it your-self. It will be all yours, and yours alone, for it is so hidden and secluded that I defy any feet but my own or whoso shall keep step with mine to find it. Shall that foot be yours, Nellie?"

Her face beamed with a bright assent. "It may be difficult to track it from here," he said, "but stand where you are a moment, and don't move, rustle, nor agitate the air in any way. The woods are still now." He turned at right angles with the trail, moved a few paces into the ferns and underbrush, and then stopped with his finger on his lips. For an instant both remained motionless; then with his intent face bent forward and both arms extended, he began to sink slowly upon one knee and one side, inclining his body with a gentle, perfectly-graduated movement until his ear almost touched the ground. Nellie watched his graceful figure breathlessly, until, like a bow unbent, he stood suddenly erect again, and beckoned to her without changing the direction of his face.

"What is it?" she asked eagerly.

"All right; I have found it," he continued, moving forward without turning his head.

"But how? What did you kneel for?" He did not reply, but taking her hand in his continued to move slowly on through the underbrush, as if obeying some magnetic attraction. "How did you find it?" again asked the half-awed girl, her voice unconsciously falling to a whisper. Still silent, Low kept his rigid face and forward tread for twenty yards further; then he stopped and released the girl's half-impatient hand. "How did you find it?" she repeated sharply.

"With my ears and nose," replied Low gravely.

"With your nose?"

"Yes; I smelt it."

Still fresh with the memory of his picturesque attitude, the young man's reply seemed to involve something more irritating to her feelings than even that absurd anticlimax. She looked at him coldly and critically, and appeared to hesitate whether to proceed. "Is it far?" she asked.

"Not more than ten minutes now, as I shall go."

"And you won't have to smell your way again?"

"No; it is quite plain now," he answered seriously, the young girl's sarcasm slipping harmlessly from his Indian stolidity. "Don't you smell it yourself?"

But Miss Nellie's thin, cold nostrils refused to take that vulgar interest.

"Nor hear it? Listen!"

"You forget I suffer the misfortune of having been brought up under a roof," she replied coldly.

"That's true," repeated Low, in all seriousness; "it's not your fault. But do you know, I sometimes think I am peculiarly sensitive to water; I feel it miles away. At night, though I may not see it or even know where it is, I am conscious of it. It is company to me when I am alone, and I seem to hear it in my dreams. There is no music as sweet to me as its song. When you sang with me that day in church, I seemed to hear it ripple in your voice. It says to me more than the birds do, more than the rarest plants I find. It seems to live with me and for me. It is my earliest recollection; I know it will be my last, for I shall die in its embrace. Do you think, Nellie," he continued, stopping short and gazing earnestly in her face—"do you think that the chiefs knew this when they called me 'Sleeping Water'?"

To Miss Nellie's several gifts I fear the gods had not added poetry. A slight knowledge of English verse of a select character, unfortunately, did not assist her in the interpretation of the young man's speech, nor relieve her from the momentary feeling that he was at times deficient in intellect. She preferred, however, to take a personal view of the question, and expressed her sarcastic regret that she had not known before that she had been indebted to the great flume and ditch at Excelsior for the pleasure of his acquaintance. This pert remark occasioned some explanation, which ended in the girl's accepting a kiss in lieu of more logical argument. Nevertheless, she was still conscious of an inward irritation—always distinct from her singular and perfectly material passion—which found vent as the difficulties of their undeviating progress through the underbrush increased. At last she lost her shoe again, and stopped short. "It's a pity your Indian friends did not christen you 'Wild Mustard' or 'Clover,'" she said satirically, "that you might have had some sympathies and longings for the open fields instead of these horrid jungles! I know we will not get back in time."

Unfortunately, Low accepted this speech literally and with his remorseless gravity. "If my name annoys you, I can get it changed by the legislature, you know, and I can find out what my father's name was, and take that. My mother, who died in giving me birth, was the daughter of a chief."

"Then your mother was really an Indian?" said Nellie, "and you are—" She stopped short.

"But I told you all this the day we first met," said Low, with grave astonishment. "Don't you remember our long talk coming from church?"

"No," said Nellie coldly, "you didn't tell me." But she was obliged to drop her eyes before the unwavering, undeniable truthfulness of his.

"You have forgotten," he said calmly; "but it is only right

you should have your own way in disposing of a name that I have cared little for; and as you're to have a share of it—"

"Yes, but it's getting late, and if we are not going forward—" interrupted the girl impatiently.

"We ARE going forward," said Low imperturbably; "but I wanted to tell you, as we were speaking on THAT subject" (Nellie looked at her watch), "I've been offered the place of botanist and naturalist in Professor Grant's survey of Mount Shasta, and if I take it—why, when I come back, darling—well—"

"But you're not going just yet," broke in Nellie, with a new expression in her face.

"No."

"Then we need not talk of it now," she said, with animation.

Her sudden vivacity relieved him. "I see what's the matter," he said gently, looking down at her feet; "these little shoes were not made to keep step with a moccasin. We must try another way." He stooped as if to secure the erring buskin, but suddenly lifted her like a child to his shoulder. "There," he continued, placing her arm round his neck, "you are clear of the ferns and brambles now, and we can go on. Are you comfortable?" He looked up, read her answer in her burning eyes and the warm lips pressed to his forehead at the roots of his straight dark hair, and again moved onward as in a mesmeric dream. But he did not swerve from his direct course, and with a final dash through the undergrowth parted the leafy curtain before the spring.

At first the young girl was dazzled by the strong light that came from a rent in the interwoven arches of the wood. The breach had been caused by the huge bulk of one of the great giants that had half fallen, and was lying at a steep angle against one of its mightiest brethren, having borne down a lesser tree in the arc of its downward path. Two of the roots, as large as younger trees, tossed their blackened and bare limbs high in the air. The spring—the insignificant cause of this vast disruption—gurgled, flashed, and sparkled at the base; the limpid baby fingers that had laid bare the foundations of that fallen column played with the still clinging rootlets, laved the fractured and twisted limbs, and, widening, filled with sleeping water the graves from which they had been torn.

"It had been going on for years, down there," said Low, pointing to a cavity from which the fresh water now slowly welled, "but it had been quickened by the rising of the subterranean springs and rivers which always occurs at a certain stage of the dry season. I remember that on that very night—for it happened a little after midnight, when all sounds are more audible—I was troubled and oppressed in my sleep by what you would call a nightmare; a feeling as if I was kept down by bonds and pinions that I longed to break. And then I heard a crash in this direction, and the first streak of morning brought me the sound and scent of water. Six months afterwards I chanced to find my way here, as I told you, and gave it your name. I did not dream that I should ever stand beside it with you, and have you christen it yourself."

He unloosened the cup from his flask, and filling it at the spring handed it to her. But the young girl leant over the pool, and pouring the water idly back said, "I'd rather put my feet in it. Mayn't I?"

"I don't understand you," he said wonderingly.

"My feet are SO hot and dusty. The water looks deliciously cool. May I?"

"Certainly."

He turned away as Nellie, with apparent unconsciousness, seated herself on the bank, and removed her shoes and stockings. When she had dabbled her feet a few moments in the pool, she said over her shoulder—

"We can talk just as well, can't we?"

"Certainly."

"Well, then, why didn't you come to church more often, and why didn't you think of telling father that you were convicted of sin and wanted to be baptized?"

"I don't know," hesitated the young man.

"Well, you lost the chance of having father convert you, baptize you, and take you into full church fellowship."

"I never thought—" he began.

"You never thought. Aren't you a Christian?"

"I suppose so."

"He supposes so! Have you no convictions—no profession?"

"But, Nellie, I never thought that you—"

"Never thought that I—what? Do you think that I could ever be anything to a man who did not believe in justification by faith, or in the covenant of church fellowship? Do you think father would let me?"

In his eagerness to defend himself he stepped to her side. But seeing her little feet shining through the dark water, like outcroppings of delicately veined quartz, he stopped embarrassed. Miss Nellie, however, leaped to one foot, and, shaking the other over the pool, put her hand on his shoulder to steady herself. "You haven't got a towel—or," she said dubiously, looking at her small handkerchief, "anything to dry them on?"

But Low did not, as she perhaps expected, offer his own handkerchief.

"If you take a bath after our fashion," he said gravely, "you must learn to dry yourself after our fashion."

Lifting her again lightly in his arms, he carried her a few steps to the sunny opening, and bade her bury her feet in the dried mosses and baked withered grasses that were bleaching in a hollow. The young girl uttered a cry of childish delight, as the soft ciliated fibres touched her sensitive skin.

"It is healing, too," continued Low; "a moccasin filled with it after a day on the trail makes you all right again."

But Miss Nellie seemed to be thinking of something else.

"Is that the way the squaws bathe and dry themselves?"

"I don't know; you forget I was a boy when I left them."

"And you're sure you never knew any?"

"None."

The young girl seemed to derive some satisfaction in moving her feet up and down for several minutes among the grasses in the hollow; then, after a pause, said, "You are quite certain I am the first woman that ever touched this spring?"

"Not only the first woman, but the first human being, except myself."

"How nice!"

They had taken each other's hands; seated side by side, they leaned against a curving elastic root that half supported, half encompassed, them. The girl's capricious, fitful manner succumbed as before to the near contact of her companion. Looking into her eyes, Low fell into a sweet, selfish lover's monologue, descriptive of his past and present feelings towards her, which she accepted with a heightened color, a slight exchange of sentiment, and a strange curiosity. The sun had painted their half-embraced silhouettes against the slanting tree-trunk, and began to decline unnoticed; the ripple of the water mingling with their whispers came as one sound to the listening ear; even their eloquent silences were as deep, and, I wot, perhaps as dangerous, as the darkened pool that filled so noiselessly a dozen yards away. So quiet were they that the tremor of invading wings once or twice shook the silence, or the quick scamper of frightened feet rustled the dead grass. But in the midst of a prolonged stillness the young man sprang up so suddenly that Nellie was still half clinging to his neck as he stood erect. "Hush!" he whispered; "some one is near!"

He disengaged her anxious hands gently, leaped upon the slanting tree-trunk, and running half-way up its incline with the agility of a squirrel, stretched himself at full length upon it and listened.

To the impatient, inexplicably startled girl, it seemed an age before he rejoined her.

"You are safe," he said; "he is going by the western trail towards Indian Spring."

"Who is HE?" she asked, biting her lips with a poorly restrained gesture of mortification and disappointment.

"Some stranger," replied Low.

"As long as he wasn't coming here, why did you give me such a fright?" she said pettishly. "Are you nervous because a single wayfarer happens to stray here?"

"It was no wayfarer, for he tried to keep near the trail," said Low. "He was a stranger to the wood, for he lost his way every now and then. He was seeking or expecting some one, for he stopped frequently and waited or listened. He had not walked far, for he wore spurs that tinkled and caught in the brush; and yet he had not ridden here, for no horse's hoofs passed the road since we have been here. He must have come from Indian Spring."

"And you heard all that when you listened just now?" asked Nellie, half disdainfully.

Impervious to her incredulity Low turned his calm eyes on her face. "Certainly, I'll bet my life on what I say. Tell me: do you know anybody in Indian Spring who would likely spy upon you?"

The young girl was conscious of a certain ill-defined uneasiness, but answered, "No."

"Then it was not YOU he was seeking," said Low

thoughtfully. Miss Nellie had not time to notice the emphasis, for he added, "You must go at once, and lest you have been followed I will show you another way back to Indian Spring. It is longer, and you must hasten. Take your shoes and stockings with you until we are out of the bush."

He raised her again in his arms and strode once more out through the covert into the dim aisles of the wood. They spoke but little; she could not help feeling that some other discordant element, affecting him more strongly than it did her, had come between them, and was half perplexed and half frightened. At the end of ten minutes he seated her upon a fallen branch, and telling her he would return by the time she had resumed her shoes and stockings glided from her like a shadow. She would have uttered an indignant protest at being left alone, but he was gone ere she could detain him. For a moment she thought she hated him. But when she had mechanically shod herself once more, not without nervous shivers at every falling needle, he was at her side.

"Do you know anyone who wears a frieze coat like that?" he asked, handing her a few torn shreds of wool affixed to a splinter of bark.

Miss Nellie instantly recognized the material of a certain sporting coat worn by Mr. Jack Brace on festive occasions, but a strange yet infallible instinct that was part of her nature made her instantly disclaim all knowledge of it.

"No," she said.

"Not anyone who scents himself with some doctor's stuff like cologne?" continued Low, with the disgust of keen olfactory sensibilities.

Again Miss Nellie recognized the perfume with which the

gallant expressman was wont to make redolent her little parlor, but again she avowed no knowledge of its possessor. "Well," returned Low with some disappointment, "such a man has been here. Be on your guard. Let us go at once."

She required no urging to hasten her steps, but hurried breathlessly at his side. He had taken a new trail by which they left the wood at right angles with the highway, two miles away. Following an almost effaced mule track along a slight depression of the plain, deep enough, however, to hide them from view, he accompanied her, until, rising to the level again, she saw they were beginning to approach the highway and the distant roofs of Indian Spring. "Nobody meeting you now," he whispered, "would suspect where you had been. Good night! until next week—remember."

They pressed each other's hands, and standing on the slight ridge outlined against the paling sky, in full view of the highway, parting carelessly, as if they had been chance met travelers. But Nellie could not restrain a parting backward glance as she left the ridge. Low had descended to the deserted trail, and was running swiftly in the direction of the Carquinez Woods.

CHAPTER IV

Teresa awoke with a start. It was day already, but how far advanced the even, unchanging, soft twilight of the woods gave no indication. Her companion had vanished, and to her bewildered senses so had the camp-fire, even to its embers and ashes. Was she awake, or had she wandered away unconsciously in the night? One glance at the tree above her dissipated the fancy. There was the opening of her quaint retreat and the hanging strips of bark, and at the foot of the opposite tree lay the carcass of the bear. It had been skinned, and, as Teresa thought with an inward shiver, already looked half its former size.

Not yet accustomed to the fact that a few steps in either direction around the circumference of those great trunks produced the sudden appearance or disappearance of any figure, Teresa uttered a slight scream as her young comp-anion unexpectedly stepped to her side. "You see a change here," he said; "the stamped-out ashes of the camp-fire lie under the brush," and he pointed to some cleverly scattered boughs and strips of bark which completely effaced the traces of last night's bivouac. "We can't afford to call the attention of any packer or hunter who might straggle this way to this particular spot and this particular tree; the more naturally," he added, "as they always prefer to camp over an old fire." Accepting this explanation meekly, as partly a reproach for her caprice of the previous night, Teresa hung her head.

"I'm very sorry," she said, "but wouldn't that," pointing to the carcass of the bear, "have made them curious?"

But Low's logic was relentless.

"By this time there would have been little left to excite curiosity, if you had been willing to leave those beasts to their work."

"I'm very sorry," repeated the woman, her lips quivering.

"They are the scavengers of the wood," he continued in a lighter tone; "if you stay here you must try to use them to keep your house clean."

Teresa smiled nervously.

"I mean that they shall finish their work to-night," he added, "and I shall build another camp-fire for us a mile from here until they do."

But Teresa caught his sleeve.

"No," she said hurriedly, "don't, please, for me. You must not take the trouble, nor the risk. Hear me; do, please. I can bear it, I WILL bear it—to-night. I would have borne it last night, but it was so strange—and"—she passed her hands over her forehead—"I think I must have been half mad. But I am not so foolish now."

She seemed so broken and despondent that he replied reassuringly: "Perhaps it would be better that I should find another hiding-place for you, until I can dispose of that carcass so that it will not draw dogs after the wolves, and men after THEM. Besides, your friend the sheriff will probably remember the bear when he remembers anything, and try to get on its track again."

"He's a conceited fool," broke in Teresa in a high voice, with a slight return of her old fury, "or he'd have guessed where that shot came from; and," she added in a lower tone, looking down at her limp and nerveless fingers, "he wouldn't have let a poor, weak, nervous wretch like me get away."

"But his deputy may put two and two together, and connect your escape with it."

Teresa's eyes flashed. "It would be like the dog, just to save his pride, to swear it was an ambush of my friends, and that he was overpowered by numbers. Oh yes! I see it all!" she almost screamed, lashing herself into a rage at the bare contemplation of this diminution of her glory. "That's the dirty lie he tells everywhere, and is telling now."

She stamped her feet and glanced savagely around, as if at any risk to proclaim the falsehood. Low turned his impassive, truthful face towards her.

"Sheriff Dunn," he began gravely, "is a politician, and a fool when he takes to the trail as a hunter of man or beast. But he is not a coward nor a liar. Your chances would be better if he were—if he laid your escape to an ambush of your friends, than if his pride held you alone responsible."

"If he's such a good man, why do you hesitate?" she replied bitterly. "Why don't you give me up at once, and do a service to one of your friends?"

"I do not even know him," returned Low opening his clear

eyes upon her. "I've promised to hide you here, and I shall hide you as well from him as from anybody."

Teresa did not reply, but suddenly dropping down upon the ground buried her face in her hands and began to sob convulsively. Low turned impassively away, and putting aside the bark curtain climbed into the hollow tree. In a few moments he reappeared, laden with provisions and a few simple cooking utensils, and touched her lightly on the shoulder. She looked up timidly; the paroxysm had passed, but her lashes yet glittered.

"Come," he said, "come and get some breakfast. I find you have eaten nothing since you have been here—twenty-four hours."

"I didn't know it," she said, with a faint smile. Then seeing his burden, and possessed by a new and strange desire for some menial employment, she said hurriedly, "Let me carry something—do, please," and even tried to disencumber him.

Half annoyed, Low at last yielded, and handing his rifle said, "There, then, take that; but be careful—it's loaded!"

A cruel blush burnt the woman's face to the roots of her hair as she took the weapon hesitatingly in her hand.

"No!" she stammered, hurriedly lifting her shame-suffused eyes to his; "no! no!"

He turned away with an impatience which showed her how completely gratuitous had been her agitation and its significance, and said, "Well, then, give it back if you are afraid of it." But she as suddenly declined to return it; and shouldering it deftly, took her place by his side. Silently they moved from the hollow tree together.

During their walk she did not attempt to invade his taciturnity. Nevertheless she was as keenly alive and watchful of his every movement and gesture as if she had hung enchanted on his lips. The unerring way with which he pursued a viewless, undeviating path through those trackless woods, his quick reconnaissance of certain trees or openings, his mute inspection of some almost imperceptible footprint of bird or beast, his critical examination of certain plants which he plucked and deposited in his deerskin haversack, were not lost on the quick-witted woman. As they gradually changed the clear, unencumbered aisles of the central woods for a more tangled undergrowth, Teresa felt that subtle admiration which culminates in imitation, and simulating perfectly the step, tread, and easy swing of her companion, followed so accurately his lead that she won a gratified exclamation from him when their goal was reached—a broken, blackened shaft, splintered by long-forgotten lightning, in the centre of a tangled carpet of wood-clover.

"I don't wonder you distanced the deputy," he said cheerfully, throwing down his burden, "if you can take the hunting-path like that. In a few days, if you stay here, I can venture to trust you alone for a little pasear when you are tired of the tree."

Teresa looked pleased, but busied herself with arrangements for the breakfast, while he gathered the fuel for the roaring fire which soon blazed beside the shattered tree.

Teresa's breakfast was a success. It was a revelation to the young nomad, whose ascetic habits and simple tastes were usually content with the most primitive forms of frontier cookery. It was at least a surprise to him to know that without extra trouble kneaded flour, water, and saleratus need not be essentially heavy; that coffee need not be boiled with sugar to the consistency of syrup; that even that rarest delicacy, small shreds of venison covered with ashes and broiled upon the end of a ramrod boldly thrust into the flames, would be better and even more expeditiously cooked upon burning coals. Moved in his practical nature, he was surprised to find this curious creature of disorganized nerves and useless impulses informed with an intelligence that did not preclude the welfare of humanity or the existence of a soul. He respected her for some minutes, until in the midst of a culinary triumph a big tear dropped and spluttered in the saucepan. But he forgave the irrelevancy by taking no notice of it, and by doing full justice to that particular dish.

Nevertheless, he asked several questions based upon these recently discovered qualities. It appeared that in the old days of her wanderings with the circus troupe she had often been forced to undertake this nomadic housekeeping. But she "despised it," had never done it since, and always had refused to do it for "him"—the personal pronoun referring, as Low understood, to her lover, Curson. Not caring to revive these memories further, Low briefly concluded: "I don't know what you were, or what you may be, but from what I see of you you've got all the sabe of a frontierman's wife."

She stopped and looked at him, and then with an impulse of imprudence that only half concealed a more serious vanity, asked, "Do you think I might have made a good squaw?"

"I don't know," he replied quietly. "I never saw enough of them to know."

Teresa, confident from his clear eyes that he spoke the truth, but having nothing ready to follow this calm disposal of her curiosity, relapsed into silence.

The meal finished, Teresa washed their scant table equipage in a little spring near the camp-fire; where, catching sight of her disordered dress and collar, she rapidly threw her shawl, after the national fashion, over her shoulder and pinned it quickly. Low cached the remaining provisions and the few cooking utensils under the dead embers and ashes, obliterating all superficial indication of their camp-fire as deftly and artistically as he had before.

"There isn't the ghost of a chance," he said in explanation, "that anybody but you or I will set foot here before we come back to supper, but it's well to be on guard. I'll take you back to the cabin now, though I bet you could find your way there as well as I can."

On their way back Teresa ran ahead of her companion, and plucking a few tiny leaves from a hidden oasis in the bark-strewn trail brought them to him.

"That's the kind you're looking for, isn't it?" she said, half timidly.

"It is," responded Low, in gratified surprise; "but how did you know it? You're not a botanist, are you?"

"I reckon not," said Teresa; "but you picked some when we came, and I noticed what they were."

Here was indeed another revelation. Low stopped and gazed at her with such frank, open, utterly unabashed curiosity that her black eyes fell before him.

"And do you think," he asked with logical deliberation, "that you could find any plant from another I should give you?"

"Yes."

"Or from a drawing of it"

"Yes; perhaps even if you described it to me."

A half-confidential, half-fraternal silence followed.

"I tell you what. I've got a book—"

"I know it," interrupted Teresa; "full of these things."

"Yes. Do you think you could—"

"Of course I could," broke in Teresa, again.

"But you don't know what I mean," said the imperturbable Low.

"Certainly I do. Why, find 'em, and preserve all the different ones for you to write under—that's it, isn't it?"

Low nodded his head, gratified but not entirely convinced that she had fully estimated the magnitude of the endeavor.

"I suppose," said Teresa, in the feminine postscriptum voice which it would seem entered even the philosophical calm of the aisles they were treading—"I suppose that SHE places great value on them?"

Low had indeed heard Science personified before, nor was it at all impossible that the singular woman walking by his side had also. He said "Yes;" but added, in mental reference to the Linnean Society of San Francisco, that "THEY were rather particular about the rarer kinds."

Content as Teresa had been to believe in Low's tender relations with some favored ONE of her sex, this frank confession of a plural devotion staggered her.

"They?" she repeated.

"Yes," he continued calmly. "The Botanical Society I correspond with are more particular than the Government Survey."

"Then you are doing this for a society?" demanded Teresa, with a stare.

"Certainly. I'm making a collection and classification of specimens. I intend—but what are you looking at?"

Teresa had suddenly turned away. Putting his hand lightly on her shoulder, the young man brought her face to face him again.

She was laughing.

"I thought all the while it was for a girl," she said; "and—" But here the mere effort of speech sent her off into an audible and genuine outburst of laughter. It was the first time he had seen her even smile other than bitterly. Characteristically unconscious of any humor in her error, he remained unembarrassed. But he could not help noticing a change in the expression of her face, her voice, and even her intonation. It seemed as if that fit of laughter had loosed the last ties that bound her to a self-imposed character, had swept away the last barrier between her and her healthier nature, had dispossessed a painful unreality, and relieved the morbid tension of a purely nervous attitude. The change in her utterance and the resumption of her softer Spanish accent seemed to have come with her confidences, and Low took leave of her before their sylvan cabin with a comrade's heartiness, and a complete forgetfulness that her voice had ever irritated him.

When he returned that afternoon he was startled to find the

cabin empty. But instead of bearing any appearance of disturbance or hurried flight, the rude interior seemed to have magically assumed a decorous order and cleanliness unknown before. Fresh bark hid the inequalities of the floor. The skins and blankets were folded in the corners, the rude shelves were carefully arranged, even a few tall ferns and bright but quickly fading flowers were disposed around the blackened chimney. She had evidently availed herself of the change of clothing he had brought her, for her late garments were hanging from the hastily-devised wooden pegs driven in the wall. The young man gazed around him with mixed feelings of gratification and uneasiness. His presence had been dispossessed in a single hour; his ten years of lonely habitation had left no trace that this woman had not effaced with a deft move of her hand. More than that, it looked as if she had always occupied it; and it was with a singular conviction that even when she should occupy it no longer it would only revert to him as her dwelling that he dropped the bark shutters athwart the opening, and left it to follow her.

To his quick ear, fine eye, and abnormal senses, this was easy enough. She had gone in the direction of this morning's camp. Once or twice he paused with a half-gesture of recognition and a characteristic "Good!" at the place where she had stopped, but was surprised to find that her main course had been as direct as his own. Deviating from this direct line with Indian precaution, he first made a circuit of the camp, and approached the shattered trunk from the opposite direction. He consequently came upon Teresa unawares. But the momentary astonishment and embarrassment were his alone.

He scarcely recognized her. She was wearing the garments he had brought her the day before—a certain discarded gown of Miss Nellie Wynn, which he had hurriedly begged from her under the pretext of clothing the wife of a distressed overland emigrant then on the way to the mines. Although he had satisfied his conscience with the intention of confessing the pious fraud to her when Teresa was gone and safe from pursuit, it was not without a sense of remorse that he witnessed the sacrilegious transformation. The two women were nearly the same height and size; and although Teresa's maturer figure accented the outlines more strongly, it was still becoming enough to increase his irritation.

Of this becomingness she was doubtless unaware at the moment that he surprised her. She was conscious of having "a change," and this had emboldened her to "do her hair" and otherwise compose herself. After their greeting she was the first to allude to the dress, regretting that it was not more of a rough disguise, and that, as she must now discard the national habit of wearing her shawl "manta" fashion over her head, she wanted a hat. "But you must not," she said, "borrow any more dresses for me from your young woman. Buy them for me at some shop. They left me enough money for that." Low gently put aside the few pieces of gold she had drawn from her pocket, and briefly reminded her of the suspicion such a purchase by him would produce. "That's so," she said, with a laugh. "Caramba! what a mule I'm becoming! Ah! wait a moment. I have it! Buy me a common felt hat—a man's hat—as if for yourself, as a change to that animal," pointing to the fox-tailed cap he wore summer and winter, "and I'll show you a trick. I haven't run a theatrical wardrobe for nothing." Nor had she, for the hat thus procured, a few days later, became, by the aid of a silk handkerchief and a bluejay's feather, a fascinating "pork pie."

Whatever cause of annoyance to Low still lingered in Teresa's dress, it was soon forgotten in a palpable evidence of Teresa's value as a botanical assistant. It appeared that during the afternoon she had not only duplicated his specimens, but had discoverd one or two rare plants as yet unclassified in the flora of the Carquinez Woods. He was delighted, and in turn, over the campfire, yielded up some details of his present life and some of his earlier recollections.

"You don't remember anything of your father?" she asked. "Did he ever try to seek you out?"

"No! Why should he?" replied the imperturbable Low; "he was not a Cherokee."

"No, he was a beast," responded Teresa promptly. "And your mother—do you remember her?"

"No, I think she died."

"You THINK she died? Don't you know?"

"No!"

"Then you're another!" said Teresa. Notwithstanding this frankness, they shook hands for the night: Teresa nestling like a rabbit in a hollow by the side of the campfire; Low with his feet towards it, Indian-wise, and his head and shoulders pillowed on his haversack, only half distinguishable in the darkness beyond.

With such trivial details three uneventful days slipped by. Their retreat was undisturbed, nor could Low detect, by the least evidence to his acute perceptive faculties, that any intruding feet had since crossed the belt of shade. The echoes of passing events at Indian Spring had recorded the escape of Teresa as occurring at a remote and purely imaginative distance, and her probable direction the county of Yolo.

"Can you remember," he one day asked her, "what time it

Bret Harte

was when you cut the riata and got away?"

Teresa pressed her hands upon her eyes and temples.

"About three, I reckon."

"And you were here at seven; you could have covered some ground in four hours?"

"Perhaps—I don't know," she said, her voice taking up its old quality again. "Don't ask me—I ran all the way."

Her face was quite pale as she removed her hands from her eyes, and her breath came as quickly as if she had just finished that race for life.

"Then you think I am safe here?" she added, after a pause.

"Perfectly—until they find you are NOT in Yolo. Then they'll look here. And THAT'S the time for you to go THERE." Teresa smiled timidly.

"It will take them some time to search Yolo—unless," she added, "you're tired of me here." The charming non sequitur did not, however, seem to strike the young man. "I've got time yet to find a few more plants for you," she suggested.

"Oh, certainly!"

"And give you a few more lessons in cooking."

"Perhaps."

The conscientious and literal Low was beginning to doubt if she were really practical. How otherwise could she trifle with such a situation?

It must be confessed that that day and the next she did trifle with it. She gave herself up to a grave and delicious languor that seemed to flow from shadow and silence and permeate her entire being. She passed hours in a thoughtful repose of mind and spirit that seemed to fall like balm from those steadfast guardians, and distill their gentle ether in her soul; or breathed into her listening ear immunity from the forgotten past, and security for the present. If there was no dream of the future in this calm, even recurrence of placid existence, so much the better. The simple details of each succeeding day, the quaint housekeeping, the brief companionship and coming and going of her young host— himself at best a crystallized personification of the sedate and hospitable woods—satisfied her feeble cravings. She no longer regretted the inferior position that her fears had obliged her to take the first night she came; she began to look up to this young man—so much younger than herself— without knowing what it meant; it was not until she found that this attitude did not detract from his picturesqueness that she discovered herself seeking for reasons to degrade him from this seductive eminence.

A week had elapsed with little change. On two days he had been absent all day, returning only in time to sup in the hollow tree, which, thanks to the final removal of the dead bear from its vicinity, was now considered a safer retreat than the exposed camp-fire. On the first of these occasions she received him with some preoccupation, paying but little heed to the scant gossip he brought from Indian Spring, and retiring early under the plea of fatigue, that he might seek his own distant camp-fire, which, thanks to her stronger nerves and regained courage, she no longer required so near. On the second occasion, he found her writing a letter more or less blotted with her tears. When it was finished, she begged him to post it at Indian Spring, where in two days an answer would be returned, under cover, to him.

"I hope you will be satisfied then," she added.

"Satisfied with what?" queried the young man.

"You'll see," she replied, giving him her cold hand. "Good-night."

"But can't you tell me now?" he remonstrated, retaining her hand.

"Wait two days longer—it isn't much," was all she vouch-safed to answer.

The two days passed. Their former confidence and good fellowship were fully restored when the morning came on which he was to bring the answer from the post-office at Indian Spring. He had talked again of his future, and had recorded his ambition to procure the appointment of naturalist to a Government Surveying Expedition. She had even jocularly proposed to dress herself in man's attire and "enlist" as his assistant.

"But you will be safe with your friends, I hope, by that time," responded Low.

"Safe with my friends," she repeated in a lower voice. "Safe with my friends—yes!" An awkward silence followed; Teresa broke it gayly: "But your girl, your sweetheart, my benefactor—will SHE let you go?"

"I haven't told her yet," said Low, gravely, "but I don't see why she should object."

"Object, indeed!" interrupted Teresa in a high voice and a sudden and utterly gratuitous indignation; "how should she? I'd like to see her do it!"

She accompanied him some distance to the intersection of the trail, where they parted in good spirits. On the dusty plain without a gale was blowing that rocked the high tree-tops above her, but, tempered and subdued, entered the low aisles with a fluttering breath of morning and a sound like the cooing of doves. Never had the wood before shown so sweet a sense of security from the turmoil and tempest of the world beyond; never before had an intrusion from the outer life— even in the shape of a letter—seemed so wicked a desecration. Tempted by the solicitation of air and shade, she lingered, with Low's herbarium slung on her shoulder.

A strange sensation, like a shiver, suddenly passed across her nerves, and left them in a state of rigid tension. With every sense morbidly acute, with every faculty strained to its utmost, the subtle instincts of Low's woodcraft transformed and possessed her. She knew it now! A new element was in the wood—a strange being—another life—another man approaching! She did not even raise her head to look about her, but darted with the precision and fleetness of an arrow in the direction of her tree. But her feet were arrested, her limbs paralzyed, her very existence suspended, by the sound of a voice:—

"Teresa!"

It was a voice that had rung in her ears for the last two years in all phases of intensity, passion, tenderness, and anger; a voice upon whose modulations, rude and unmusical though they were, her heart and soul had hung in transport or anguish. But it was a chime that had rung its last peal to her senses as she entered the Carquinez Woods, and for the last week had been as dead to her as a voice from the grave. It was the voice of her lover—Dick Curson!

CHAPTER V

The wind was blowing towards the stranger, so that he was nearly upon her when Teresa first took the alarm. He was a man over six feet in height, strongly built, with a slight tendency to a roundness of bulk which suggested reserved rather than impeded energy. His thick beard and mustache were closely cropped around a small and handsome mouth that lisped except when he was excited, but always kept fellowship with his blue eyes in a perpetual smile of half-cynical good-humor. His dress was superior to that of the locality; his general expression that of a man of the world, albeit a world of San Francisco, Sacramento, and Murderer's Bar. He advanced towards her with a laugh and an outstretched hand.

"YOU here!" she gasped, drawing back.

Apparently neither surprised nor mortified at this reception, he answered frankly, "Yeth. You didn't expect me, I know. But Doloreth showed me the letter you wrote her, and—well—here I am, ready to help you, with two men and a thpare horthe waiting outside the woodth on the blind trail."

"You—YOU—here?" she only repeated.

Curson shrugged his shoulders. "Yeth. Of courth you never

expected to thee me again, and leatht of all HERE. I'll admit that; I'll thay I wouldn't if I'd been in your plathe. I'll go further, and thay you didn't want to thee me again— anywhere. But it all cometh to the thame thing; here I am. I read the letter you wrote Doloreth. I read how you were hiding here, under Dunn'th very nothe, with his whole pothe out, cavorting round and barkin' up the wrong tree. I made up my mind to come down here with a few nathty friends of mine and cut you out under Dunn'th nothe, and run you over into Yuba—that'th all."

"How dared she show you my letter—YOU of all men? How dared she ask YOUR help?" continued Teresa, fiercely.

"But she didn't athk my help," he responded coolly. "D—d if I don't think she jutht calculated I'd be glad to know you were being hunted down and thtarving, that I might put Dunn on your track."

"You lie!" said Teresa, furiously; "she was my friend. A better friend than those who professed—more," she added, with a contemptuous drawing away of her skirt as if she feared Curson's contamination.

"All right. Thettle that with her when you go back," continued Curson philosophically. "We can talk of that on the way. The thing now ith to get up and get out of thethe woods. Come!"

Teresa's only reply was a gesture of scorn.

"I know all that," continued Curson half soothingly, "but they're waiting."

"Let them wait. I shall not go."

"What will you do?"

"Stay here—till the wolves eat me."

"Teresa, listen. D—it all—Teresa—Tita! see here," he said with sudden energy. "I swear to God it's all right. I'm willing to let by-gones be by-gones and take a new deal. You shall come back as if nothing had happened, and take your old place as before. I don't mind doing the square thing, all round. If that's what you mean, if that's all that stands in the way, why, look upon the thing as settled. There, Tita, old girl, come."

Careless or oblivious of her stony silence and starting eyes, he attempted to take her hand. But she disengaged herself with a quick movement, drew back, and suddenly crouched like a wild animal about to spring. Curson folded his arms as she leaped to her feet; the little dagger she had drawn from her garter flashed menacingly in the air, but she stopped.

The man before her remained erect, impassive, and silent; the great trees around and beyond her remained erect, impassive, and silent; there was no sound in the dim aisles but the quick panting of her mad passion, no movement in the calm, motionless shadow but the trembling of her uplifted steel. Her arm bent and slowly sank, her fingers relaxed, the knife fell from her hand.

"That'th quite enough for a thow," he said, with a return to his former cynical ease and a perceptible tone of relief in his voice. "It'th the thame old Theretha. Well, then, if you won't go with me, go without me; take the led horthe and cut away. Dick Athley and Petereth will follow you over the county line. If you want thome money, there it ith." He took a buckskin purse from his pocket. "If you won't take it from me"—he hesitated as she made no reply—"Athley'th flush and ready to lend you thome."

She had not seemed to hear him, but had stooped in some embarrassment, picked up the knife and hastily hid it, then with averted face and nervous fingers was beginning to tear strips of loose bark from the nearest trunk.

"Well, what do you thay?"

"I don't want any money, and I shall stay here." She hesitated, looked around her, and then added, with an effort, "I suppose you meant well. Be it so! Let by-gones be by-gones. You said just now, 'It's the same old Teresa.' So she is, and seeing she's the same she's better here than anywhere else."

There was enough bitterness in her tone to call for Curson's half-perfunctory sympathy.

"That be d—d," he responded quickly. "Jutht thay you'll come, Tita, and—"

She stopped his half-spoken sentence with a negative gesture. "You don't understand. I shall stay here."

"But even if they don't theek you here, you can't live here forever. The friend that you wrote about who wath tho good to you, you know, can't keep you here alwayth; and are you thure you can alwayth trutht her?"

"It isn't a woman; it's a man." She stopped short, and colored to the line of her forehead. "Who said it was a woman?" she continued fiercely, as if to cover her confusion with a burst of gratuitous anger. "Is that another of your lies?"

Curson's lips, which for a moment had completely lost their

smile, were now drawn together in a prolonged whistle. He gazed curiously at her gown, at her hat, at the bow of bright ribbon that tied her black hair, and said, "Ah!"

"A poor man who has kept my secret," she went on hurriedly—"a man as friendless and lonely as myself. Yes," disregarding Curson's cynical smile, "a man who has shared everything—"

"Naturally," suggested Curson.

"And turned himself out of his only shelter to give me a roof and covering," she continued mechanically, struggling with the new and horrible fancy that his words awakened.

"And thlept every night at Indian Thpring to save your reputation," said Curson. "Of courthe."

Teresa turned very white. Curson was prepared for an outburst of fury—perhaps even another attack. But the crushed and beaten woman only gazed at him with frightened and imploring eyes. "For God's sake, Dick, don't say that!"

The amiable cynic was staggered. His good-humor and a certain chivalrous instinct he could not repress got the better of him. He shrugged his shoulders. "What I thay, and what you DO, Teretha, needn't make us quarrel. I've no claim on you—I know it. Only—" a vivid sense of the ridiculous, powerful in men of his stamp, completed her victory—"only don't thay anything about my coming down here to cut you out from the—the—THE SHERIFF." He gave utterance to a short but unaffected laugh, made a slight grimace, and turned to go.

Teresa did not join in his mirth. Awkward as it would have

been if he had taken a severer view of the subject, she was mortified even amidst her fears and embarrassment at his levity. Just as she had become convinced that his jealousy had made her over-conscious, his apparent good-humored indifference gave that over-consciousness a guilty significance. Yet this was lost in her sudden alarm as her companion, looking up, uttered an exclamation, and placed his hand upon his revolver. With a sinking conviction that the climax had come, Teresa turned her eyes. From the dim aisles beyond, Low was approaching. The catastrophe seemed complete.

She had barely time to utter an imploring whisper: "In the name of God, not a word to him." But a change had already come over her companion. It was no longer a parley with a foolish woman; he had to deal with a man like himself. As Low's dark face and picturesque figure came nearer, Mr. Curson's proposed method of dealing with him was made audible.

"Ith it a mulatto or a Thircuth, or both?" he asked, with affected anxiety.

Low's Indian phlegm was impervious to such assault. He turned to Teresa, without apparently noticing her companion. "I turned back," he said quietly, "as soon as I knew there were strangers here; I thought you might need me." She noticed for the first time that, in addition to his rifle, he carried a revolver and hunting knife in his belt.

"Yeth," returned Curson, with an ineffectual attempt to imitate Low's phlegm; "but ath I didn't happen to be a sthranger to this lady, perhaps it wathn't nethethary, particularly ath I had two friends—"

"Waiting at the edge of the wood with a led horse,"

76   Bret Harte

interrupted Low, without addressing him, but apparently continuing his explanation to Teresa. But she turned to Low with feverish anxiety.

"That's so—he is an old friend—" she gave a quick, imploring glance at Curson—"an old friend who came to help me away—he is very kind," she stammered, turning alternately from the one to the other; "but I told him there was no hurry—at least to-day—that you—were—very good—too, and would hide me a little longer, until your plan—you know YOUR plan," she added, with a look of beseeching significance to Low—"could be tried." And then, with a helpless conviction that her excuses, motives, and emotions were equally and perfectly transparent to both men, she stopped in a tremble.

"Perhapth it 'th jutht ath well, then, that the gentleman came thtraight here, and didn't tackle my two friendth when he pathed them," observed Curson, half sarcastically.

"I have not passed your friends, nor have I been near them," said Low, looking at him for the first time, with the same exasperating calm, "or perhaps I should not be HERE or they THERE. I knew that one man entered the wood a few moments ago, and that two men and four horses remained outside."

"That's true," said Teresa to Curson excitedly—"that's true. He knows all. He can see without looking, hear without listening. He—he—" she stammered, colored, and stopped.

The two men had faced each other. Curson, after his first good-natured impulse, had retained no wish to regain Teresa, whom he felt he no longer loved, and yet who, for that very reason perhaps, had awakened his chivalrous instincts. Low, equally on his side, was altogether unconscious of any feeling which might grow into a passion, and prevent him from letting her go with another if for her own safety. They were both men of a certain taste and refinement. Yet, in spite of all this, some vague instinct of the baser male animal remained with them, and they were moved to a mutually aggressive attitude in the presence of the female.

One word more, and the opening chapter of a sylvan Iliad might have begun. But this modern Helen saw it coming, and arrested it with an inspiration of feminine genius. Without being observed, she disengaged her knife from her bosom and let it fall as if by accident. It struck the ground with the point of its keen blade, bounded and rolled between them. The two men started and looked at each other with a foolish air. Curson laughed.

"I reckon she can take care of herthelf," he said, extending his hand to Low. "I'm off. But if I'm wanted SHE'LL know where to find me." Low took the proffered hand, but neither of the two men looked at Teresa. The reserve of antagonism once broken, a few words of caution, advice, and encouragement passed between them, in apparent obliviousness of her presence or her personal responsibility. As Curson at last nodded a farewell to her, Low insisted upon accompanying him as far as the horses, and in another moment she was again alone.

She had saved a quarrel between them at the sacrifice of herself, for her vanity was still keen enough to feel that this exhibition of her old weakness had degraded her in their eyes, and, worse, had lost the respect her late restraint had won from Low. They had treated her like a child or a crazy woman, perhaps even now were exchanging criticisms upon her—perhaps pitying her! Yet she had prevented a quarrel, a fight; possibly the death of either one or the other of these men who despised her, for none better knew than she the trivial beginning and desperate end of these encounters. Would they—would Low ever realize it, and forgive her? Her small, dark hands went up to her eyes and she sank upon the ground. She looked through tear-veiled lashes upon the mute and giant witnesses of her deceit and passion, and tried to draw, from their immovable calm, strength and consolation as before. But even they seemed to stand apart, reserved and forbidding.

When Low returned she hoped to gather from his eyes and manner what had passed between him and her former lover. But beyond a mere gentle abstraction at times he retained his usual calm. She was at last forced to allude to it herself with simulated recklessness.

"I suppose I didn't get a very good character from my last place?" she said, with a laugh.

"I don't understand you," he replied, in evident sincerity.

She bit her lip and was silent. But as they were returning home, she said gently, "I hope you were not angry with me for the lie I told when I spoke of 'your plan.' I could not give the real reason for not returning with—with—that man. But it's not all a lie. I have a plan—if you haven't. When you are ready to go to Sacramento to take your place, dress me as an Indian boy, paint my face, and let me go with you. You can leave me—there—you know."

"It's not a bad idea," he responded gravely. "We will see."

On the next day, and the next, the rencontre seemed to be forgotten. The herbarium was already filled with rare specimens. Teresa had even overcome her feminine repugnance to "bugs" and creeping things so far as to assist in his entomological collection. He had drawn from a sacred cache in the hollow of a tree the few worn text-books from which he had studied.

"They seem very precious," she said, with a smile.

"Very," he replied gravely. "There was one with plates that the ants ate up, and it will be six months before I can afford to buy another."

Teresa glanced hurriedly over his well-worn buckskin suit, at his calico shirt with its pattern almost obliterated by countless washings, and became thoughtful.

"I suppose you couldn't buy one at Indian Spring?" she said innocently.

For once Low was startled out of his phlegm. "Indian Spring!" he ejaculated; "perhaps not even in San Francisco. These came from the States."

"How did you get them?" persisted Teresa.

"I bought them for skins I got over the ridge."

"I didn't mean that—but no matter. Then you mean to sell that bearskin, don't you?" she added.

Low had, in fact, already sold it, the proceeds having been invested in a gold ring for Miss Nellie, which she scrupulously did not wear except in his presence. In his singular truthfulness he would have frankly confessed it to Teresa, but the secret was not his own. He contented himself with saying that he had disposed of it at Indian Spring.

Teresa started, and communicated unconsciously some of her nervousness to her companion. They gazed in each other's eyes with a troubled expression.

"Do you think it was wise to sell that particular skin, which might be identified?" she asked timidly.

Low knitted his arched brows, but felt a strange sense of relief. "Perhaps not," he said carelessly; "but it's too late now to mend matters."

That afternoon she wrote several letters, and tore them up. One, however, she retained, and handed it to Low to post at Indian Spring, whither he was going. She called his attention to the superscription, being the same as the previous letter, and added, with affected gayety, "But if the answer isn't as prompt, perhaps it will be pleasanter than the last." Her quick feminine eye noticed a little excitement in his manner and a more studious attention to his dress. Only a few days before she would not have allowed this to pass without some mischievous allusion to his mysterious sweetheart; it troubled her greatly now to find that she could not bring herself to this household pleasantry, and that her lip trembled and her eye grew moist as he parted from her.

The afternoon passed slowly; he had said he might not return to supper until late, nevertheless a strange restlessness took possession of her as the day wore on. She put aside her work, the darning of his stockings, and rambled aimlessly through the woods. She had wandered she knew not how far, when she was suddenly seized with the same vague sense of a foreign presence which she had felt before. Could it be Curson again, with a word of warning? No! she knew it was not he; so subtle had her sense become that she even fancied that she detected in the invisible aura projected by the unknown no significance or relation to herself or Low, and felt no fear. Nevertheless she deemed it wisest to seek the protection of her sylvan bower, and hurried swiftly thither.

But not so quickly nor directly that she did not once or twice pause in her flight to examine the new-comer from behind a friendly trunk. He was a stranger—a young fellow with a brown mustache, wearing heavy Mexican spurs in his riding-boots, whose tinkling he apparently did not care to conceal. He had perceived her, and was evidently pursuing her, but so awkwardly and timidly that she eluded him with ease. When she had reached the security of the hollow tree and pulled the curtain of bark before the narrow opening, with her eye to the interstices, she waited his coming. He arrived breathlessly in the open space before the tree where the bear once lay; the dazed, bewildered, and half-awed expression of his face, as he glanced around him and through the openings of the forest aisles, brought a faint smile to her saddened face. At last he called in a half-embarrassed voice:—

"Miss Nellie!"

The smile faded from Teresa's cheek. Who was "Miss Nellie?" She pressed her ear to the opening. "Miss Wynn!" the voice again called, but was lost in the echoless woods. Devoured with a new gratuitous curiosity, in another moment Teresa felt she would have disclosed herself at any risk, but the stranger rose and began to retrace his steps. Long after his tinkling spurs were lost in the distance, Teresa remained like a statue, staring at the place where he had stood. Then she suddenly turned like a mad woman, glanced down at the gown she was wearing, tore it from her back as if it had been a polluted garment, and stamped upon it in a convulsion of rage. And then, with her beautiful bare arms clasped together over her head, she threw herself upon her couch in a tempest of tears.

CHAPTER VI

When Miss Nellie reached the first mining extension of Indian Spring, which surrounded it like a fosse, she descended for one instant into one of its trenches, opened her parasol, removed her duster, hid it under a bowlder, and with a few shivers and cat-like strokes of her soft hands not only obliterated all material traces of the stolen cream of Carquinez Woods, but assumed a feline demureness quite inconsistent with any moral dereliction. Unfortunately, she forgot to remove at the same time a certain ring from her third finger, which she had put on with her duster and had worn at no other time. With this slight exception, the benignant fate which always protected that young person brought her in contact with the Burnham girls at one end of the main street as the returning coach to Excelsior entered the other, and enabled her to take leave of them before the coach office with a certain ostentation of parting which struck Mr. Jack Brace, who was lingering at the doorway, into a state of utter bewilderment.

Here was Miss Nellie Wynn, the belle of Excelsior, calm, quiet, self-possessed, her chaste cambric skirts and dainty shoes as fresh as when she had left her father's house; but where was the woman of the brown duster, and where the yellow-dressed apparition of the woods? He was feebly repeating to himself his mental adjuration of a few hours before when he caught her eye, and was taken with a blush and a fit of coughing. Could he have been such an egregious fool, and was it not plainly written on his embarrassed face for her to read?

"Are we going down together?" asked Miss Nellie with an exceptionally gracious smile.

There was neither affectation nor coquetry in this advance. The girl had no idea of Brace's suspicion of her, nor did any uneasy desire to placate or deceive a possible rival of Low's prompt her graciousness. She simply wished to shake off in this encounter the already stale excitement of the past two hours, as she had shaken the dust of the woods from her clothes. It was characteristic of her irresponsible nature and transient susceptibilities that she actually enjoyed the relief of change; more than that, I fear, she looked upon this infidelity to a past dubious pleasure as a moral principle. A mild, open flirtation with a recognized man like Brace, after her secret passionate tryst with a nameless nomad like Low, was an ethical equipoise that seemed proper to one of her religious education.

Brace was only too happy to profit by Miss Nellie's condescension; he at once secured the seat by her side, and spent the four hours and a half of their return journey to Excelsior in blissful but timid communion with her. If he did not dare to confess his past suspicions, he was equally afraid to venture upon the boldness he had premeditated a few hours before. He was therefore obliged to take a middle course of slightly egotistical narration of his own personal adventures, with which he beguiled the young girl's ear. This he only departed from once, to describe to her a valuable grizzly bearskin which he had seen that day for sale at Indian Spring, with a view to divining her possible acceptance of it for a "buggy robe;" and once to comment upon a ring which she had inadvertently disclosed in pulling off her glove.

"It's only an old family keepsake," she added, with easy mendacity; and affecting to recognize in Mr. Brace's curiosity a not unnatural excuse for toying with her charming fingers, she hid them in chaste and virginal seclusion in her lap, until she could recover the ring and resume her glove.

A week passed—a week of peculiar and desiccating heat for even those dry Sierra table-lands. The long days were filled with impalpable dust and acrid haze suspended in the motionless air; the nights were breathless and dewless; the cold wind which usually swept down from the snow line was laid to sleep over a dark monotonous level, whose horizon was pricked with the eating fires of burning forest crests. The lagging coach of Indian Spring drove up at Excelsior, and precipitated its passengers with an accompanying cloud of dust before the Excelsior Hotel. As they emerged from the coach, Mr. Brace, standing in the doorway, closely scanned their begrimed and almost unrecognizable faces. They were the usual type of travelers: a single professional man in dusty black, a few traders in tweeds and flannels, a sprinkling of miners in red and gray shirts, a Chinaman, a negro, and a Mexican packer or muleteer. This latter for a moment mingled with the crowd in the bar-room, and even penetrated the corridor and dining-room of the hotel, as if impelled by a certain semi-civilized curiosity, and then strolled with a lazy, dragging step—half impeded by the enormous leather leggings, chains, and spurs, peculiar to his class—down the main street. The darkness was gathering, but the muleteer indulged in the same childish scrutiny of the dimly lighted shops, magazines, and saloons, and even of the occasional groups of citizens at the street corners. Apparently young, as far as the outlines of his figure could be seen, he seemed to show even more than the usual concern of masculine Excelsior in the charms of womankind. The few female figures about at that hour, or visible at window or veranda, received his marked attention; he respectfully followed the two auburn-haired daughters of Deacon Johnson on their way to choir meeting to the door of the church. Not content with that act of discreet gallantry, after they had entered he managed to slip unperceived behind them.

The memorial of the Excelsior gamblers' generosity was a modern building, large and pretentious, for even Mr. Wynn's popularity, and had been good-humoredly known, in the characteristic language of the generous donors, as one of the "biggest religious bluffs" on record. Its groined rafters, which were so new and spicy that they still suggested their native forest aisles, seldom covered more than a hundred devotees, and in the rambling choir, with its bare space for the future organ, the few choristers, gathered round a small harmonium, were lost in the deepening shadow of that summer evening. The muleteer remained hidden in the obscurity of the vestibule. After a few moments' desultory conversation, in which it appeared that the unexpected absence of Miss Nellie Wynn, their leader, would prevent their practicing, the choristers withdrew. The stranger, who had listened eagerly, drew back in the darkness as they passed out, and remained for a few moments a vague and motionless figure in the silent church. Then coming cautiously to the window, the flapping broad-brimmed hat was put aside, and the faint light of the dying day shone in the black eyes of Teresa! Despite her face, darkened with dye and disfigured with dust, the matted hair piled and twisted around her head, the strange dress and boyish figure, one swift glance from under her raised lashes betrayed her identity.

She turned aside mechanically into the first pew, picked up and opened a hymn-book. Her eyes became riveted on a name written on the title-page, "Nellie Wynn." HER name, and HER book. The instinct that had guided her here was right; the slight gossip of her fellow-passengers was right; this was the clergyman's daughter, whose praise filled all mouths. This was the unknown girl the stranger was seeking, but who in turn perhaps had been seeking Low—the girl who absorbed his fancy—the secret of his absences, his preoccupation, his coldness! This was the girl whom to see, perhaps in his arms, she was now periling her liberty and her life unknown to him! A slight odor, some faint perfume of its owner, came from the book; it was the same she had noticed in the dress Low had given her. She flung the volume to the ground, and, throwing her arms over the back of the pew before her, buried her face in her hands.

In that light and attitude she might have seemed some rapt acolyte abandoned to self-communion. But whatever yearning her soul might have had for higher sympathy or deeper consolation, I fear that the spiritual Tabernacle of Excelsior and the Reverend Mr. Wynn did not meet that requirement. She only felt the dry, oven-like heat of that vast shell, empty of sentiment and beauty, hollow in its pretense and dreary in its desolation. She only saw in it a chief altar for the glorification of this girl who had absorbed even the pure worship of her companion, and converted and degraded his sublime paganism to her petty creed. With a woman's withering contempt for her own art displayed in another woman, she thought how she herself could have touched him with the peace that the majesty of their woodland aisles—so unlike this pillared sham—had taught her own passionate heart, had she but dared. Mingling with this imperfect theology, she felt she could have proved to him also that a brunette and a woman of her experience was better than an immature blonde. She began to loathe herself for coming hither, and dreaded to meet his face. Here a sudden thought struck her. What if he had not come here? What if she had been mistaken? What if her rash interpretation of his absence from the wood that night was simple madness? What if he should return—if he had already returned? She rose to her feet, whitening yet joyful with the thought. She could return at once; what was the girl to her now? Yet there was time to satisfy herself if he were at HER house. She had been told where it was; she could find it in the dark; an open door or window would betray some sign or sound of the occupants. She rose, replaced her hat over her eyes, knotted her flaunting scarf around her throat, groped her way to the door, and glided into the outer darkness.

CHAPTER VII

It was quite dark when Mr. Jack Brace stopped before Father Wynn's open door. The windows were also invitingly open to the wayfarer, as were the pastoral counsels of Father Wynn, delivered to some favored guest within, in a tone of voice loud enough for a pulpit. Jack Brace paused. The visitor was the convalescent sheriff, Jim Dunn, who had publicly commemorated his recovery by making his first call upon the father of his inamorata. The Reverend Mr. Wynn had been expatiating upon the unremitting heat of a possible precursor of forest fires, and exhibiting some catholic knowledge of the designs of a Deity in that regard, and what should be the policy of the Legislature, when Mr. Brace concluded to enter. Mr. Wynn and the wounded man, who occupied an arm-chair by the window, were the only occupants of the room. But in spite of the former's ostentatious greeting, Brace could see that his visit was inopportune and unwelcome. The sheriff nodded a quick, impatient recognition, which, had it not been accompanied by an anathema on the heat, might have been taken as a personal insult. Neither spoke of Miss Nellie, although it was patent to Brace that they were momentarily expecting her. All of which went far to strengthen a certain wavering purpose in his mind.

"Ah, ha! strong language, Mr. Dunn," said Father Wynn,

referring to the sheriff's adjuration, "but 'out of the fullness of the heart the mouth speaketh.' Job, sir, cursed, we are told, and even expressed himself in vigorous Hebrew regarding his birthday. Ha, ha! I'm not opposed to that. When I have often wrestled with the spirit I confess I have sometimes said, 'D—n you.' Yes, sir, 'D—n you.'"

There was something so unutterably vile in the reverend gentleman's utterance and emphasis of this oath that the two men, albeit both easy and facile blasphemers, felt shocked; as the purest of actresses is apt to overdo the rakishness of a gay Lothario, Father Wynn's immaculate conception of an imprecation was something terrible. But he added, "The law ought to interfere with the reckless use of camp-fires in the woods in such weather by packers and prospectors."

"It isn't so much the work of white men," broke in Brace, "as it is of Greasers, Chinamen, and Diggers, especially Diggers. There's that blasted Low, ranges the whole Carquinez Woods as if they were his. I reckon he ain't particular just where he throws his matches."

"But he's not a Digger; he's a Cherokee, and only a half-breed at that," interpolated Wynn. "Unless," he added, with the artful suggestion of the betrayed trust of a too credulous Christian, "he deceived me in this as in other things."

In what other things Low had deceived him he did not say; but, to the astonishment of both men, Dunn growled a dissent to Brace's proposition. Either from some secret irritation with that possible rival, or impatience at the prolonged absence of Nellie, he had "had enough of that sort of hog-wash ladled out to him for genuine liquor." As to the Carquinez Woods, he [Dunn] "didn't know why Low hadn't as much right there as if he'd grabbed it under a preemption law and didn't live there." With this hint at certain speculations of Father Wynn in public lands for a homestead, he added that "If they [Brace and Wynn] could bring him along any older American settler than an Indian, they might rake down his [Dunn's] pile." Unprepared for this turn in the conversation, Wynn hastened to explain that he did not refer to the pure aborigine, whose gradual extinction no one regretted more than himself, but to the mongrel, who inherited only the vices of civilization. "There should be a law, sir, against the mingling of races. There are men, sir, who violate the laws of the Most High by living with Indian women—squaw men, sir, as they are called."

Dunn rose with a face livid with weakness and passion. "Who dares say that? They are a d—d sight better than sneaking Northern Abolitionists, who married their daughters to buck niggers like—" But a spasm of pain withheld this Parthian shot at the politics of his two companions, and he sank back helplessly in his chair.

An awkward silence ensued. The three men looked at each other in embarrassment and confusion. Dunn felt that he had given way to a gratuitous passion; Wynn had a vague presentiment that he had said something that imperiled his daughter's prospects; and Brace was divided between an angry retort and the secret purpose already alluded to.

"It's all the blasted heat," said Dunn, with a forced smile, pushing away the whisky which Wynn had ostentatiously placed before him.

"Of course," said Wynn hastily; "only it's a pity Nellie ain't here to give you her smelling-salts. She ought to be back now," he added, no longer mindful of Brace's presence; "the coach is over-due now, though I reckon the heat made Yuba Bill take it easy at the up grade."

"If you mean the coach from Indian Spring," said Brace quietly, "it's in already; but Miss Nellie didn't come on it."

"May be she got out at the Crossing," said Wynn cheerfully; "she sometimes does."

"She didn't take the coach at Indian Spring," returned Brace, "because I saw it leave, and passed it on Buckskin ten minutes ago, coming up the hills."

"She's stopped over at Burnham's," said Wynn reflectively. Then, in response to the significant silence of his guests, he added, in a tone of chagrin which his forced heartiness could not disguise, "Well, boys, it's a disappointment all round; but we must take the lesson as it comes. I'll go over to the coach office and see if she's sent any word. Make yourselves at home until I return."

When the door had closed behind him, Brace arose and took his hat as if to go. With his hand on the lock, he turned to his rival, who, half hidden in the gathering darkness, still seemed unable to comprehend his ill-luck.

"If you're waiting for that bald-headed fraud to come back with the truth about his daughter," said Brace coolly, "you'd better send for your things and take up your lodgings here."

"What do you mean?" said Dunn sternly.

"I mean that she's not at the Burnhams'; I mean that he either does or does not know WHERE she is, and that in either case he is not likely to give you information. But I can."

"You can?"

"Yes."

"Then, where is she?"

"In the Carquinez Woods, in the arms of the man you were just defending—Low, the half-breed."

The room had become so dark that from the road nothing could be distinguished. Only the momentary sound of struggling feet was heard.

"Sit down," said Brace's voice, "and don't be a fool. You're too weak, and it ain't a fair fight. Let go your hold. I'm not lying—I wish to God I was!"

There was silence, and Brace resumed, "We've been rivals, I know. May be I thought my chance as good as yours. If what I say ain't truth, we'll stand as we stood before; and if you're on the shoot, I'm your man when you like, where you like, or on sight if you choose. But I can't bear to see another man played upon as I've been played upon—given dead away as I've been. It ain't on the square.

"There," he continued, after a pause, "that's right, now steady. Listen. A week ago that girl went down just like this to Indian Spring. It was given out, like this, that she went to the Burnhams'. I don't mind saying, Dunn, that I went down myself, all on the square, thinking I might get a show to talk to her, just as YOU might have done, you know, if you had my chance. I didn't come across her anywhere. But two men that I met thought they recognized her in a disguise going into the woods. Not suspecting anything, I went after her; saw her at a distance in the middle of the woods in another dress that I can swear to, and was just coming up to her when she vanished—went like a squirrel up a tree, or down like a gopher in the ground, but vanished."

"Is that all?" said Dunn's voice. "And just because you were a d—d fool, or had taken a little too much whisky, you thought—"

"Steady. That's just what I said to myself," interrupted Brace coolly, "particularly when I saw her that same afternoon in another dress, saying 'Good-by' to the Burnhams, as fresh as a rose and as cold as those snow-peaks. Only one thing—she had a ring on her finger she never wore before, and didn't expect me to see."

"What if she did? She might have bought it. I reckon she hasn't to consult you," broke in Dunn's voice sternly.

"She didn't buy it," continued Brace quietly. "Low gave that Jew trader a bearskin in exchange for it, and presented it to her. I found that out two days afterwards. I found out that out of the whole afternoon she spent less than an hour with the Burnhams. I found out that she bought a duster like the disguise the two men saw her in. I found the yellow dress she wore that day hanging up in Low's cabin—the place where I saw her go—THE RENDEZVOUS WHERE SHE MEETS HIM. Oh, you're listenin', are you? Stop! SIT DOWN!

"I discovered it by accident," continued the voice of Brace when all was again quiet; "it was hidden as only a squirrel or an Injin can hide when they improve upon nature. When I was satisfied that the girl had been in the woods, I was determined to find out where she vanished, and went there again. Prospecting around, I picked up at the foot of one of the biggest trees this yer old memorandum-book, with grasses and herbs stuck in it. I remembered that I'd heard old Wynn say that Low, like the d—d Digger that he was, collected these herbs; only he pretended it was for science. I reckoned the book was his and that he mightn't be far away. I lay low and waited. Bimeby I saw a lizard running down the root. When he got sight of me he stopped."

"D—n the lizard! What's that got to do with where she is now?"

"Everything. That lizard had a piece of sugar in his mouth. Where did it come from? I made him drop it, and calculated he'd go back for more. He did. He scooted up that tree and slipped in under some hanging strips of bark. I shoved 'em aside, and found an opening to the hollow where they do their housekeeping."

"But you didn't see her there—and how do you know she is there now?"

"I determined to make it sure. When she left to-day, I started an hour ahead of her, and hid myself at the edge of the woods. An hour after the coach arrived at Indian Spring, she came there in a brown duster and was joined by him. I'd have followed them, but the d—d hound has the ears of a squirrel, and though I was five hundred yards from him he was on his guard."

"Guard be blessed! Wasn't you armed? Why didn't you go for him?" said Dunn, furiously.

"I reckoned I'd leave that for you," said Brace coolly. "If he'd killed me, and if he'd even covered me with his rifle, he'd been sure to let daylight through me at double the distance. I shouldn't have been any better off, nor you either. If I'd killed HIM, it would have been your duty as sheriff to put me in jail; and I reckon it wouldn't have broken your heart, Jim Dunn, to have got rid of TWO rivals instead of one. Hullo! Where are you going?"

"Going?" said Dunn hoarsely. "Going to the Carquinez Woods, by God! to kill him before her. I'LL risk it, if you daren't. Let me succeed, and you can hang ME and take the girl yourself."

"Sit down, sit down. Don't be a fool, Jim Dunn! You wouldn't keep the saddle a hundred yards. Did I say I wouldn't help you? No. If you're willing, we'll run the risk together, but it must be in my way. Hear me. I'll drive you down there in a buggy before daylight, and we'll surprise them in the cabin or as they leave the wood. But you must come as if to arrest him for some offense—say, as an escaped Digger from the Reservation, a dangerous tramp, a destroyer of public property in the forests, a suspected road agent, or anything to give you the right to hunt him. The exposure of him and Nellie, don't you see, must be accidental. If he resists, kill him on the spot, and nobody'll blame you; if he goes peaceably with you, and you once get him in Excelsior jail, when the story gets out that he's taken the belle of Excelsior for his squaw, if you'd the angels for your posse you couldn't keep the boys from hanging him to the first tree. What's that?"

He walked to the window, and looked out cautiously.

"If it was the old man coming back and listening," he said, after a pause, "it can't he helped. He'll hear it soon enough, if he don't suspect something already."

"Look yer, Brace," broke in Dunn hoarsely. "D—d if I understand you or you me. That dog Low has got to answer to ME, not to the LAW! I'll take my risk of killing him, on sight and on the square. I don't reckon to handicap myself with a warrant, and I am not going to draw him out with a lie. You hear me? That's me all the time!"

"Then you calkilate to go down thar," said Brace contemptuously, "yell out for him and Nellie, and let him line you on a rest from the first tree as if you were a grizzly."

There was a pause. "What's that you were saying just now about a bearskin he sold?" asked Dunn slowly, as if reflecting.

"He exchanged a bearskin," replied Brace, "with a single hole right over the heart. He's a dead shot, I tell you."

"D—n his shooting," said Dunn. "I'm not thinking of that. How long ago did he bring in that bearskin?"

"About two weeks, I reckon. Why?"

"Nothing! Look yer, Brace, you mean well—thar's my hand. I'll go down with you there, but not as the sheriff. I'm going there as Jim Dunn, and you can come along as a white man, to see things fixed on the square. Come!"

Brace hesitated. "You'll think better of my plan before you get there; but I've said I'd stand by you, and I will. Come, then. There's no time to lose."

They passed out into the darkness together.

"What are you waiting for?" said Dunn impatiently, as Brace, who was supporting him by the arm, suddenly halted at the corner of the house.

"Some one was listening—did you not see him? Was it the old man?" asked Brace hurriedly.

"Blast the old man! It was only one of them Mexican packers chock-full of whisky, and trying to hold up the house. What are you thinking of? We shall be late."

In spite of his weakness, the wounded man hurriedly urged Brace forward, until they reached the latter's lodgings. To his surprise, the horse and buggy were already before the door.

"Then you reckoned to go, any way?" said Dunn, with a searching look at his companion.

"I calkilated SOMEBODY would go," returned Brace, evasively, patting the impatient Buckskin; "but come in and take a drink before we leave."

Dunn started out of a momentary abstraction, put his hand on his hip, and mechanically entered the house. They had scarcely raised the glasses to their lips when a sudden rattle of wheels was heard in the street. Brace set down his glass and ran to the window.

"It's the mare bolted," he said, with an oath. "We've kept her too long standing. Follow me," and he dashed down the staircase into the street. Dunn followed with difficulty; when he reached the door he was already confronted by his breathless companion. "She's gone off on a run, and I'll swear there was a man in the buggy!" He stopped and examined the halter-strap, still fastened to the fence. "Cut! by God!"

Dunn turned pale with passion. "Who's got another horse and buggy?" he demanded.

"The new blacksmith in Main Street; but we won't get it by borrowing," said Brace.

"How then?" asked Dunn savagely.

"Seize it, as the sheriff of Yuba and his deputy, pursuing a confederate of the Injin Low—THE HORSE THIEF!"

CHAPTER VIII

The brief hour of darkness that preceded the dawn was that night intensified by a dense smoke, which, after blotting out horizon and sky, dropped a thick veil on the high road and the silent streets of Indian Spring. As the buggy containing Sheriff Dunn and Brace dashed through the obscurity, Brace suddenly turned to his companion.

"Some one ahead!"

The two men bent forward over the dashboard. Above the steady plunging of their own horse-hoofs they could hear the quicker irregular beat of other hoofs in the darkness before them.

"It's that horse thief!" said Dunn, in a savage whisper. "Bear to the right, and hand me the whip."

A dozen cuts of the cruel lash, and their maddened horse, bounding at each stroke, broke into a wild canter. The frail vehicle swayed from side to side at each spring of the elastic shafts. Steadying himself by one hand on the low rail, Dunn drew his revolver with the other. "Sing out to him to pull up, or we'll fire. My voice is clean gone," he added, in a husky whisper.

They were so near that they could distinguish the bulk of a vehicle careering from side to side in the blackness ahead. Dunn deliberately raised his weapon. "Sing out!" he repeated impatiently. But Brace, who was still keeping in the shadow, suddenly grasped his companion's arm.

"Hush! It's NOT Buckskin," he whispered hurriedly.

"Are you sure?"

"DON'T YOU SEE WE'RE GAINING ON HIM?" replied the other contemptuously. Dunn grasped his companion's hand and pressed it silently. Even in that supreme moment this horseman's tribute to the fugitive Buckskin forestalled all baser considerations of pursuit and capture!

In twenty seconds they were abreast of the stranger, crowding his horse and buggy nearly into the ditch; Brace keenly watchful, Dunn suppressed and pale. In half a minute they were leading him a length; and when their horse again settled down to his steady work, the stranger was already lost in the circling dust that followed them. But the victors seemed disappointed. The obscurity had completely hidden all but the vague outlines of the mysterious driver.

"He's not our game, anyway," whispered Dunn. "Drive on."

"But if it was some friend of his," suggested Brace uneasily, "what would you do?"

"What I SAID I'd do," responded Dunn savagely. "I don't want five minutes to do it in, either; we'll be half an hour ahead of that d——d fool, whoever he is. Look here; all you've got to do is to put me in the trail to that cabin. Stand back of me, out of gun-shot, alone, if you like, as my deputy, or with any number you can pick up as my posse. If he gets by me as

Nellie's lover, you may shoot him or take him as a horse thief, if you like."

"Then you won't shoot him on sight?"

"Not till I've had a word with him."

"But—"

"I've chirped," said the sheriff gravely. "Drive on."

For a few moments only the plunging hoofs and rattling wheels were heard. A dull, lurid glow began to define the horizon. They were silent until an abatement of the smoke, the vanishing of the gloomy horizon line, and a certain impenetrability in the darkness ahead showed them they were nearing the Carquinez Woods. But they were surprised on entering them to find the dim aisles alight with a faint mystic Aurora. The tops of the towering spires above them had caught the gleam of the distant forest fires, and reflected it as from a gilded dome.

"It would be hot work if the Carquinez Woods should conclude to take a hand in this yer little game that's going on over on the Divide yonder," said Brace, securing his horse and glancing at the spires overhead. "I reckon I'd rather take a back seat at Injin Spring when the show commences."

Dunn did not reply, but, buttoning his coat, placed one hand on his companion's shoulder, and sullenly bade him "lead the way." Advancing slowly and with difficulty the desperate man might have been taken for a peaceful invalid returning from an early morning stroll. His right hand was buried thoughtfully in the side pocket of his coat. Only Brace knew that it rested on the handle of his pistol.

From time to time the latter stopped and consulted the faint trail with a minuteness that showed recent careful study. Suddenly he paused. "I made a blaze hereabouts to show where to leave the trail. There it is," he added, pointing to a slight notch cut in the trunk of an adjoining tree.

"But we've just passed one," said Dunn, "if that's what you are looking after, a hundred yards back."

Brace uttered an oath, and ran back in the direction signified by his companion. Presently he returned with a smile of triumph.

"They've suspected something. It's a clever trick, but it won't hold water. That blaze which was done to muddle you was cut with an axe; this which I made was done with a bowie-knife. It's the real one. We're not far off now. Come on."

They proceeded cautiously, at right angles with the "blazed" tree, for ten minutes more. The heat was oppressive; drops of perspiration rolled from the forehead of the sheriff, and at times, when he attempted to steady his uncertain limbs, his hands shrank from the heated, blistering bark he touched with ungloved palms.

"Here we are," said Brace, pausing at last. "Do you see that biggest tree, with the root stretching out halfway across to the opposite one?"

"No, it's further to the right and abreast of the dead brush," interrupted Dunn quickly, with a sudden revelation that this was the spot where he had found the dead bear in the night Teresa escaped.

"That's so," responded Brace, in astonishment.

"And the opening is on the other side, opposite the dead brush," said Dunn.

"Then you know it?" said Brace suspiciously.

"I reckon!" responded Dunn, grimly. "That's enough! Fall back!"

To the surprise of his companion, he lifted his head erect, and with a strong, firm step walked directly to the tree. Reaching it, he planted himself squarely before the opening.

"Halloo!" he said.

There was no reply. A squirrel scampered away close to his feet. Brace, far in the distance, after an ineffectual attempt to distinguish his companion through the intervening trunks, took off his coat, leaned against a tree, and lit a cigar.

"Come out of that cabin!" continued Dunn, in a clear, resonant voice. "Come out before I drag you out!"

"All right, 'Captain Scott.' Don't shoot, and I'll come down," said a voice as clear and as high as his own. The hanging strips of bark were dashed aside, and a woman leaped lightly to the ground.

Dunn staggered back. "Teresa! by the Eternal!"

It was Teresa! the old Teresa! Teresa, a hundred times more vicious, reckless, hysterical, extravagant, and outrageous than before. Teresa, staring with tooth and eye, sunburnt and embrowned, her hair hanging down her shoulders, and her shawl drawn tightly around her neck.

"Teresa it is! the same old gal! Here we are again! Return of the favorite in her original character! For two weeks only! Houp la! Tshk!" and, catching her yellow skirt with her fingers, she pirouetted before the astounded man, and ended in a pose. Recovering himself with an effort, Dunn dashed forward and seized her by the wrist.

"Answer me, woman! Is that Low's cabin?"

"It is."

"Who occupies it besides?"

"I do."

"And who else?"

"Well," drawled Teresa slowly, with an extravagant affectation of modesty, "nobody else but us, I reckon. Two's company, you know, and three's none."

"Stop! Will you swear that there isn't a young girl, his—his sweetheart—concealed there with you?"

The fire in Teresa's eye was genuine as she answered steadily, "Well, it ain't my style to put up with that sort of thing; at least, it wasn't over at Yolo, and you know it, Jim Dunn, or I wouldn't be here."

"Yes, yes," said Dunn hurriedly. "But I'm a d—d fool, or worse, the fool of a fool. Tell me, Teresa, is this man Low your lover?"

Teresa lowered her eyes as if in maidenly confusion. "Well, if I'd known that YOU had any feeling of your own about it—if you'd spoken sooner—"

"Answer me, you devil!"

"He is."

"And he has been with you here—yesterday—to-night?"

"He has."

"Enough." He laughed a weak, foolish laugh, and, turning pale, suddenly lapsed against a tree. He would have fallen, but with a quick instinct Teresa sprang to his side, and supported him gently to a root. The action over, they both looked astounded.

"I reckon that wasn't much like either you or me," said Dunn slowly, "was it? But if you'd let me drop then you'd have stretched out the biggest fool in the Sierras." He paused, and looked at her curiously. "What's come over you; blessed if I seem to know you now."

She was very pale again, and quiet; that was all.

"Teresa! d—n it, look here! When I was laid up yonder in Excelsior I said I wanted to get well for only two things. One was to hunt you down, the other to marry Nellie Wynn. When I came here I thought that last thing could never be. I came here expecting to find her here with Low, and kill him—perhaps kill her too. I never once thought of you; not once. You might have risen up before me—between me and him—and I'd have passed you by. And now that I find it's all a mistake, and it was you, not her, I was looking for, why—"

"Why," she interrupted bitterly, "you'll just take me, of course, to save your time and earn your salary. I'm ready."

"But I'M not, just yet," he said faintly. "Help me up."

She mechanically assisted him to his feet.

"Now stand where you are," he added, "and don't move beyond this tree till I return."

He straightened himself with an effort, clenched his fists until the nails were nearly buried in his palms, and strode with a firm, steady step in the direction he had come. In a few moments he returned and stood before her.

"I've sent away my deputy—the man who brought me here, the fool who thought you were Nellie. He knows now he made a mistake. But who it was he mistook for Nellie he does not know, nor shall ever know, nor shall any living being know, other than myself. And when I leave the wood to-day I shall know it no longer. You are safe here as far as I am concerned, but I cannot screen you from others prying. Let Low take you away from here as soon as he can."

"Let him take me away? Ah, yes. For what?"

"To save you," said Dunn. "Look here, Teresa! Without knowing it, you lifted me out of hell just now, and because of the wrong I might have done her—for HER sake, I spare you and shirk my duty."

"For her sake!" gasped the woman—"for her sake! Oh, yes! Go on."

"Well," said Dunn gloomily, "I reckon perhaps you'd as lieve left me in hell, for all the love you bear me. And may be you've grudge enough agin me still to wish I'd found her and him together."

"You think so?" she said, turning her head away.

"There, d—n it! I didn't mean to make you cry. May be you wouldn't, then. Only tell that fellow to take you out of this, and not run away the next time he sees a man coming."

"He didn't run," said Teresa, with flashing eyes. "I—I—I sent him away," she stammered. Then, suddenly turning with fury upon him, she broke out, "Run! Run from you! Ha, ha! You said just now I'd a grudge against you. Well, listen, Jim Dunn. I'd only to bring you in range of that young man's rifle, and you'd have dropped in your tracks like—"

"Like that bar, the other night," said Dunn, with a short laugh. "So THAT was your little game?" He checked his laugh suddenly—a cloud passed over his face. "Look here, Teresa," he said, with an assumption of carelessness that was as transparent as it was utterly incompatible with his frank, open selfishness. "What became of that bar? The skin—eh? That was worth something?"

"Yes," said Teresa quietly. "Low exchanged it and got a ring for me from that trader Isaacs. It was worth more, you bet. And the ring didn't fit either—"

"Yes," interrupted Dunn, with an almost childish eagerness.

"And I made him take it back, and get the value in money. I hear that Isaacs sold it again and made another profit; but that's like those traders." The disingenuous candor of Teresa's manner was in exquisite contrast to Dunn. He rose and grasped her hand so heartily she was forced to turn her eyes away.

"Good-by!" he said.

"You look tired," she murmured, with a sudden gentleness that surprised him; "let me go with you a part of the way."

"It isn't safe for you just now," he said, thinking of the possible consequences of the alarm Brace had raised.

"Not the way YOU came," she replied; "but one known only to myself."

He hesitated only a moment. "All right, then," he said finally, "let us go at once. It's suffocating here, and I seem to feel this dead bark crinkle under my feet."

She cast a rapid glance around her, and then seemed to sound with her eyes the far-off depths of the aisles, beginning to grow pale with the advancing day, but still holding a strange quiver of heat in the air. When she had finished her half-abstracted scrutiny of the distance, she cast one backward glance at her own cabin and stopped.

"Will you wait a moment for me?" she asked gently.

"Yes—but—no tricks, Teresa! It isn't worth the time."

She looked him squarely in the eyes without a word.

"Enough," he said; "go!"

She was absent for some moments. He was beginning to become uneasy, when she made her appearance again, clad in her old faded black dress. Her face was very pale, and her eyes were swollen, but she placed his hand on her shoulder, and bidding him not to fear to lean upon her, for she was quite strong, led the way.

"You look more like yourself now, and yet—blast it all!— you don't either," said Dunn, looking down upon her. "You've changed in some way. What is it? Is it on account of that Injin? Couldn't you have found a white man in his place?"

"I reckon he's neither worse nor better for that," she replied bitterly; "and perhaps he wasn't as particular in his taste as a white man might have been. But," she added, with a sudden spasm of her old rage, "it's a lie; he's NOT an Indian, no more than I am. Not unless being born of a mother who scarcely knew him, of a father who never even saw him, and being brought up among white men and wild beasts—less cruel than they were—could make him one!"

Dunn looked at her in surprise not unmixed with admiration. "If Nellie," he thought, "could but love ME like that!" But he only said:

"For all that, he's an Injin. Why, look at his name. It ain't Low. It's L'Eau Dormante, Sleeping Water, an Injin name."

"And what does that prove?" returned Teresa. "Only that Indians clap a nick-name on any stranger, white or red, who may camp with them. Why, even his own father, a white man, the wretch who begot him and abandoned him,—HE had an Indian name—Loup Noir."

"What name did you say?"

"Le Loup Noir, the Black Wolf. I suppose you'd call him an Indian, too? Eh! What's the matter? We're walking too fast. Stop a moment and rest. There—there, lean on me!"

She was none too soon; for, after holding him upright a moment, his limbs failed, and stooping gently she was obliged to support him half reclining against a tree.

"Its the heat!" he said. "Give me some whisky from my flask. Never mind the water," he added faintly, with a forced laugh, after he had taken a draught at the strong spirit. "Tell me more about the other water—the Sleeping Water—you know. How do you know all this about him and his—father?"

"Partly from him and partly from Curson, who wrote to me about him," she answered with some hesitation.

But Dunn did not seem to notice this incongruity of correspondence with a former lover. "And HE told you?"

"Yes; and I saw the name on an old memorandum book he has, which he says belonged to his father. It's full of old accounts of some trading post on the frontier. It's been missing for a day or two, but it will turn up. But I can swear I saw it."

Dunn attempted to rise to his feet. "Put your hand in my pocket," he said in a hurried whisper. "No, there!—bring out a book. There, I haven't looked at it yet. Is that it?" he added, handing her the book Brace had given him a few hours before.

"Yes," said Teresa, in surprise. "Where did you find it?"

"Never mind! Now let me see it, quick. Open it, for my sight is failing. There—thank you—that's all!"

"Take more whisky," said Teresa, with a strange anxiety creeping over her. "You are faint again."

"Wait! Listen, Teresa—lower—put your ear lower. Listen! I came near killing that chap Low to-day. Wouldn't it have been ridiculous?"

He tried to smile, but his head fell back. He had fainted.

CHAPTER IX

For the first time in her life Teresa lost her presence of mind in an emergency. She could only sit staring at the helpless man, scarcely conscious of his condition, her mind filled with a sudden prophetic intuition of the significance of his last words. In the light of that new revelation she looked into his pale, haggard face for some resemblance to Low, but in vain. Yet her swift feminine instinct met the objection. "It's the mother's blood that would show," she murmured, "not this man's."

Recovering herself, she began to chafe his hands and temples, and moistened his lips with the spirit. When his respiration returned with a faint color to his cheeks, she pressed his hands eagerly and leaned over him.

"Are you sure?" she asked.

"Of what?" he whispered faintly.

"That Low is really your son?"

"Who said so?" he asked, opening his round eyes upon her.

"You did yourself, a moment ago," she said quickly. "Don't you remember?"

"Did I?"

"You did. Is it not so?"

He smiled faintly. "I reckon."

She held her breath in expectation. But only the ludicrousness of the discovery seemed paramount to his weakened faculties. "Isn't it just about the ridiculousest thing all round?" he said, with a feeble chuckle. "First YOU nearly kill me before you know I am Low's father; then I'm just spoilin' to kill him before I know he's my son; then that godforsaken fool Jack Brace mistakes you for Nellie and Nellie for you. Ain't it just the biggest thing for the boys to get hold of? But we must keep it dark until after I marry Nellie, don't you see? Then we'll have a good time all round, and I'll stand the drinks. Think of it, Teresha! You don' no me, I do' no you, nobody knowsh anybody elsh. I try kill Lo'. Lo' wants kill Nellie. No thath no ri—'" but the potent liquor, overtaking his exhausted senses, thickened, impeded, and at last stopped his speech. His head slipped to her shoulder, and he became once more unconscious.

Teresa breathed again. In that brief moment she had abandoned herself to a wild inspiration of hope which she could scarcely define. Not that it was entirely a wild inspiration; she tried to reason calmly. What if she revealed the truth to him? What if she told the wretched man before her that she had deceived him; that she had overheard his conversation with Brace; that she had stolen Brace's horse to bring Low warning; that, failing to find Low in his accustomed haunts, or at the campfire, she had left a note for him pinned to the herbarium, imploring him to fly with his companion from the danger that was coming; and that, remaining on watch, she had seen them both—Brace and Dunn—approaching, and had prepared to meet them at the cabin? Would this miserable and maddened man understand her self-abnegation? Would he forgive Low and Nellie?— she did not ask for herself. Or would the revelation turn his brain, if it did not kill him outright? She looked at the sunken orbits of his eyes and hectic on his cheek, and shuddered.

Why was this added to the agony she already suffered? She had been willing to stand between them with her life, her liberty, and even—the hot blood dyed her cheek at the thought—with the added shame of being thought the cast-off mistress of that man's son. Yet all this she had taken upon herself in expiation of something—she knew not clearly what; no, for nothing—only for HIM. And yet this very situation offered her that gleam of Hope which had thrilled her; a hope so wild in its improbability, so degrading in its possibility, that at first she knew not whether despair was not preferable to its shame. And yet was it unreasonable? She was no longer passionate; she would be calm and think it out fairly.

She would go to Low at once. She would find him some-where—and even if with that girl, what mattered?—and she would tell him all. When he knew that the life and death of his father lay in the scale, would he let his brief, foolish passion for Nellie stand in the way? Even if he were not influenced by filial affection or mere compassion, would his pride let him stoop to a rivalry with the man who had deserted his youth? Could he take Dunn's promised bride, who must have coquetted with him to have brought him to this miserable plight? Was this like the calm, proud young god she knew? Yet she had an uneasy instinct that calm, proud young gods and goddesses did things like this, and felt the weakness of her reasoning flush her own conscious cheek.

"Teresa!"

She started. Dunn was awake, and was gazing at her curiously.

"I was reckoning it was the only square thing for Low to stop this promiscuous picnicking here and marry you out and out."

"Marry me!" said Teresa in a voice that, with all her efforts, she could not make cynical.

"Yes," he repeated, "after I've married Nellie; tote you down to San Angeles, and there take my name like a man, and give it to you. Nobody'll ask after TERESA, sure—you bet your life. And if they do, and he can't stop their jaw, just you call on the old man. It's mighty queer, ain't it, Teresa, to think of your being my daughter-in-law?"

It seemed here as if he was about to lapse again into unconsciousness over the purely ludicrous aspect of the subject, but he haply recovered his seriousness. "He'll have as much money from me as he wants to go into business with. What's his line of business, Teresa?" asked this prospective father-in-law, in a large, liberal way.

"He is a botanist!" said Teresa, with a sudden childish animation that seemed to keep up the grim humor of the paternal suggestion; "and oh, he is too poor to buy books! I sent for one or two for him myself, the other day—" she hesitated—"it was all the money I had, but it wasn't enough for him to go on with his studies."

Dunn looked at her sparkling eyes and glowing cheeks, and became thoughtful. "Curson must have been a d—d fool," he said finally.

Teresa remained silent. She was beginning to be impatient

and uneasy, fearing some mischance that might delay her dreaded, yet longed-for meeting with Low. Yet she could not leave this sick and exhausted man, HIS FATHER, now bound to her by more than mere humanity.

"Couldn't you manage," she said gently, "to lean on me a few steps further, until I could bring you to a cooler spot and nearer assistance?"

He nodded. She lifted him almost like a child to his feet. A spasm of pain passed over his face. "How far is it?" he asked.

"Not more than ten minutes," she replied.

"I can make a spurt for that time," he said coolly, and began to walk slowly but steadily on. Only his face, which was white and set, and the convulsive grip of his hand on her arm betrayed the effort. At the end of ten minutes she stopped. They stood before the splintered, lightning-scarred shaft in the opening of the woods, where Low had built her first camp-fire. She carefully picked up the herbarium, but her quick eye had already detected in the distance, before she had allowed Dunn to enter the opening with her, that her note was gone. Low had been there before them; he had been warned, as his absence from the cabin showed; he would not return there. They were free from interruption—but where had he gone?

The sick man drew a long breath of relief as she seated him in the clover-grown hollow where she had slept the second night of her stay. "It's cooler than those cursed woods," he said. "I suppose it's because it's a little like a grave. What are you going to do now?" he added, as she brought a cup of water and placed it at his side.

"I am going to leave you here for a little while," she said

cheerfully, but with a pale face and nervous hands. "I'm going to leave you while I seek Low."

The sick man raised his head. "I'm good for a spurt, Teresa, like that I've just got through, but I don't think I'm up to a family party. Couldn't you issue cards later on?"

"You don't understand," she said. "I'm going to get Low to send some one of your friends to you here. I don't think he'll begrudge leaving HER a moment for that," she added to herself bitterly.

"What's that you're saying?" he queried, with the nervous quickness of an invalid.

"Nothing—but that I'm going now." She turned her face aside to hide her moistened eyes. "Wish me good luck, won't you?" she asked, half sadly, half pettishly.

"Come here!"

She came and bent over him. He suddenly raised his hands, and, drawing her face down to his own, kissed her forehead.

"Give that to HIM," he whispered, "from ME."

She turned and fled, happily for her sentiment, not hearing the feeble laugh that followed, as Dunn, in sheer imbecility, again referred to the extravagant ludicrousness of the situation. "It is about the biggest thing in the way of a sell all round," he repeated, lying on his back, confidentially to the speck of smoke-obscured sky above him. He pictured himself repeating it, not to Nellie—her severe propriety might at last overlook the fact, but would not tolerate the joke—but to her father! It would be one of those characteristic Californian jokes Father Wynn would admire.

To his exhaustion fever presently succeeded, and he began to grow restless. The heat too seemed to invade his retreat, and from time to time the little patch of blue sky was totally obscured by clouds of smoke. He amused himself with watching a lizard who was investigating a folded piece of paper, whose elasticity gave the little creature lively apprehensions of its vitality. At last he could stand the stillness of his retreat and his supine position no longer, and rolled himself out of the bed of leaves that Teresa had so carefully prepared for him. He rose to his feet stiff and sore, and, supporting himself by the nearest tree, moved a few steps from the dead ashes of the camp-fire. The movement frightened the lizard, who abandoned the paper and fled. With a satirical recollection of Brace and his "ridiculous" discovery through the medium of this animal, he stooped and picked up the paper. "Like as not," he said to himself, with grim irony, "these yer lizards are in the discovery business. P'r'aps this may lead to another mystery," and he began to unfold the paper with a smile. But the smile ceased as his eye suddenly caught his own name.

A dozen lines were written in pencil on what seemed to be a blank leaf originally torn from some book. He trembled so that he was obliged to sit down to read these words:—

"When you get this keep away from the woods. Dunn and another man are in deadly pursuit of you and your companion. I overheard their plan to surprise you in our cabin. DON'T GO THERE, and I will delay them and put them off the scent. Don't mind me. God bless you, and if you never see me again think sometimes of

"TERESA."

His trembling ceased; he did not start, but rose in an abstracted way, and made a few deliberate steps in the direction Teresa had gone. Even then he was so confused that he was obliged to refer to the paper again, but with so little effect that he could only repeat the last words, "think sometimes of Teresa." He was conscious that this was not all; he had a full conviction of being deceived, and knew that he held the proof in his hand, but he could not formulate it beyond that sentence. "Teresa"—yes, he would think of her. She would explain it. And here she was returning.

In that brief interval her face and manner had again changed. Her face was pale and quite breathless. She cast a swift glance at Dunn and the paper he mechanically held out, walked up to him, and tore it from his hand.

"Well," she said hoarsely, "what are you going to do about it?"

He attempted to speak, but his voice failed him. Even then he was conscious that if he had spoken he would have only repeated, "think sometimes of Teresa." He looked longingly but helplessly at the spot where she had thrown the paper, as if it had contained his unuttered words.

"Yes," she went on to herself, as if he was a mute, indifferent spectator—"yes, they're gone. That ends it all. The game's played out. Well!" suddenly turning upon him, "now you know it all. Your Nellie WAS here with him, and is with him now. Do you hear? Make the most of it; you've lost them—but here I am."

"Yes," he said eagerly—"yes, Teresa."

She stopped, stared at him; then taking him by the hand led him like a child back to his couch. "Well," she said, in half-savage explanation, "I told you the truth when I said the girl wasn't at the cabin last night, and that I didn't know her.

What are you glowerin' at? No! I haven't lied to you, I swear to God, except in one thing. Did you know what that was? To save him I took upon me a shame I don't deserve. I let you think I was his mistress. You think so now, don't you? Well, before God to-day—and He may take me when He likes—I'm no more to him than a sister! I reckon your Nellie can't say as much."

She turned away, and with the quick, impatient stride of some caged animal made the narrow circuit of the opening, stopping a moment mechanically before the sick man, and again, without looking at him, continuing her monotonous round. The heat had become excessive, but she held her shawl with both hands drawn tightly over her shoulders. Suddenly a wood-duck darted out of the covert blindly into the opening, struck against the blasted trunk, fell half stunned near her feet, and then, recovering, fluttered away. She had scarcely completed another circuit before the irruption was followed by a whirring bevy of quail, a flight of jays, and a sudden tumult of wings swept through the wood like a tornado. She turned inquiringly to Dunn, who had risen to his feet, but the next moment she caught convulsively at his wrist; a wolf had just dashed through the underbrush not a dozen yards away, and on either side of them they could hear the scamper and rustle of hurrying feet like the outburst of a summer shower. A cold wind arose from the opposite direction, as if to contest this wild exodus, but it was followed by a blast of sickening heat. Teresa sank at Dunn's feet in an agony of terror.

"Don't let them touch me!" she gasped; "keep them off! Tell me, for God's sake, what has happened!"

He laid his hand firmly on her arm, and lifted her in his turn to her feet like a child. In that supreme moment of physical danger, his strength, reason, and manhood returned in their plenitude of power. He pointed coolly to the trail she had quitted, and said,

"The Carquinez Woods are on fire!"

CHAPTER X

The nest of the tuneful Burnhams, although in the suburbs of Indian Spring, was not in ordinary weather and seasons hidden from the longing eyes of the youth of that settlement. That night, however, it was veiled in the smoke that encompassed the great highway leading to Excelsior. It is presumed that the Burnham brood had long since folded their wings, for there was no sign of life nor movement in the house as a rapidly-driven horse and buggy pulled up before it. Fortunately, the paternal Burnham was an early bird, in the habit of picking up the first stirring mining worm, and a resounding knock brought him half dressed to the street door. He was startled at seeing Father Wynn before him, a trifle flushed and abstracted.

"Ah ha! up betimes, I see, and ready. No sluggards here—ha, ha!" he said heartily, slamming the door behind him, and by a series of pokes in the ribs genially backing his host into his own sitting-room. "I'm up, too, and am here to see Nellie. She's here, eh—of course?" he added, darting a quick look at Burnham.

But Mr. Burnham was one of those large, liberal Western husbands who classified his household under the general title of "woman folk," for the integers of which he was not responsible. He hesitated, and then propounded over the balusters to the upper story the direct query—

"You don't happen to have Nellie Wynn up there, do ye?"

There was an interval of inquiry proceeding from half a dozen reluctant throats, more or less cottony and muffled, in those various degrees of grievance and mental distress which indicate too early roused young womanhood. The eventual reply seemed to be affirmative, albeit accompanied with a suppressed giggle, as if the young lady had just been discovered as an answer to an amusing conundrum.

"All right," said Wynn, with an apparent accession of boisterous geniality. "Tell her I must see her, and I've only got a few minutes to spare. Tell her to slip on anything and come down; there's no one here but myself, and I've shut the front door on Brother Burnham. Ha, ha!" and suiting the action to the word, he actually bundled the admiring Brother Burnham out on his own doorstep. There was a light pattering on the staircase, and Nellie Wynn, pink with sleep, very tall, very slim, hastily draped in a white counterpane with a blue border and a general classic suggestion, slipped into the parlor. At the same moment her father shut the door behind her, placed one hand on the knob, and with the other seized her wrist.

"Where were you yesterday?" he asked.

Nellie looked at him, shrugged her shoulders, and said, "Here."

"You were in the Carquinez Woods with Low Dorman; you went there in disguise; you've met him there before. He is your clandestine lover; you have taken pledges of affection from him; you have—"

"Stop!" she said.

He stopped.

"Did he tell you this?" she asked, with an expression of disdain.

"No; I overheard it. Dunn and Brace were at the house waiting for you. When the coach did not bring you, I went to the office to inquire. As I left our door I thought I saw somebody listening at the parlor windows. It was only a drunken Mexican muleteer leaning against the house; but if HE heard nothing, I did. Nellie, I heard Brace tell Dunn that he had tracked you in your disguise to the woods—do you hear? that when you pretended to be here with the girls you were with Low—alone; that you wear a ring that Low got of a trader here; that there was a cabin in the woods—"

"Stop!" she repeated.

Wynn again paused.

"And what did YOU do?" she asked.

"I heard they were starting down there to surprise you and him together, and I harnessed up and got ahead of them in my buggy."

"And found me here," she said, looking full into his eyes.

He understood her and returned the look. He recognized the full importance of the culminating fact conveyed in her words, and was obliged to content himself with its logical and worldly significance. It was too late now to take her to task for mere filial disobedience; they must become allies.

"Yes," he said hurriedly; "but if you value your reputation, if you wish to silence both these men, answer me fully."

"Go on," she said.

"Did you go to the cabin in the woods yesterday?"

"No."

"Did you ever go there with Low?"

"No; I do not know even where it is."

Wynn felt that she was telling the truth. Nellie knew it; but as she would have been equally satisfied with an equally efficacious falsehood, her face remained unchanged.

"And when did he leave you?"

"At nine o'clock, here. He went to the hotel."

"He saved his life, then, for Dunn is on his way to the woods to kill him."

The jeopardy of her lover did not seem to affect the young girl with alarm, although her eyes betrayed some interest.

"Then Dunn has gone to the woods?" she said thoughtfully.

"He has," replied Wynn.

"Is that all?" she asked.

"I want to know what you are going to do?"

"I WAS going back to bed."

"This is no time for trifling, girl."

"I should think not," she said, with a yawn; "it's too early, or too late."

Wynn grasped her wrist more tightly. "Hear me! Put whatever face you like on this affair, you are compromised —and compromised with a man you can't marry."

"I don't know that I ever wanted to marry Low, if you mean him," she said quietly.

"And Dunn wouldn't marry you now."

"I'm not so sure of that, either."

"Nellie," said Wynn excitedly, "do you want to drive me mad? Have you nothing to say—nothing to suggest?"

"Oh, you want me to help you, do you! Why didn't you say that first? Well, go and bring Dunn here."

"Are you mad? The man has gone already in pursuit of your lover, believing you with him."

"Then he will the more readily come and talk with me without him. Will you take the invitation—yes or no?"

"Yes, but—"

"Enough. On your way there you will stop at the hotel and give Low a letter from me."

"Nellie!"

"You shall read it, of course," she said scornfully, "for it will be your text for the conversation you will have with him. Will you please take your hand from the lock and open the door?"

Wynn mechanically opened the door. The young girl flew up-stairs. In a very few moments she returned with two notes: one contained a few lines of formal invitation to Dunn; the other read as follows:

"DEAR MR. DORMAN,—My father will tell you how deeply I regret that our recent botanical excursions in the Carquinez Woods have been a source of serious misapprehensions to those who had a claim to my consideration, and that I shall be obliged to discontinue them for the future. At the same time he wishes me to express my gratitude for your valuable instruction and assistance in that pleasing study, even though approaching events may compel me to relinquish it for other duties. May I beg you to accept the inclosed ring as a slight recognition of my obligations to you?

"Your grateful pupil,

"NELLIE WYNN."

When he had finished reading the letter, she handed him a ring, which he took mechanically. He raised his eyes to hers with perfectly genuine admiration. "You're a good girl, Nellie," he said, and, in a moment of parental forgetfulness, unconsciously advanced his lips towards her cheek. But she drew back in time to recall him to a sense of that human weakness.

"I suppose I'll have time for a nap yet," she said, as a gentle hint to her embarrassed parent. He nodded and turned towards the door.

"If I were you," she continued, repressing a yawn, "I'd manage to be seen on good terms with Low at the hotel; so perhaps you need not give the letter to him until the last thing. Good-by."

The sitting-room door opened and closed behind her as she slipped up-stairs, and her father, without the formality of leave-taking, quietly let himself out by the front door.

When he drove into the high road again, however, an overlooked possibility threatened for a moment to indefinitely postpone his amiable intentions regarding Low. The hotel was at the further end of the settlement towards the Carquinez Woods, and as Wynn had nearly reached it he was recalled to himself by the sounds of hoofs and wheels rapidly approaching from the direction of the Excelsior turnpike. Wynn made no doubt it was the sheriff and Brace. To avoid recognition at that moment, he whipped up his horse, intending to keep the lead until he could turn into the first cross-road. But the coming travelers had the fleetest horse, and finding it impossible to distance them he drove close to the ditch, pulling up suddenly as the strange vehicle was abreast of him, and forcing them to pass him at full speed, with the result already chronicled. When they had vanished in the darkness, Mr. Wynn, with a heart overflowing with Christian thankfulness and universal benevolence, wheeled round, and drove back to the hotel he had already passed. To pull up at the veranda with a stentorian shout, to thump loudly at the deserted bar, to hilariously beat the panels of the landlord's door, and commit a jocose assault and battery upon that half-dresssed and half-awakened man, was eminently characteristic of Wynn, and part of his amiable plans that morning.

"Something to wash this wood smoke from my throat, Brother Carter, and about as much again to prop open your eyes," he said, dragging Carter before the bar, "and glasses round for as many of the boys as are up and stirring after a hard-working Christian's rest. How goes the honest publican's trade, and who have we here?"

"Thar's Judge Robinson and two lawyers from Sacramento, Dick Curson over from Yolo," said Carter, "and that ar young Injin yarb doctor from the Carquinez Woods. I reckon he's jist up—I noticed a light under his door as I passed."

"He's my man for a friendly chat before breakfast," said Wynn. "You needn't come up. I'll find the way. I don't want a light; I reckon my eyes ain't as bright nor as young as his, but they'll see almost as far in the dark—he! he!" And, nodding to Brother Carter, he strode along the passage, and with no other introduction than a playful and preliminary "Boo!" burst into one of the rooms. Low, who by the light of a single candle was bending over the plates of a large quarto, merely raised his eyes and looked at the intruder. The young man's natural imperturbability, always exasperating to Wynn, seemed accented that morning by contrast with his own over-acted animation.

"Ah ha!—wasting the midnight oil instead of imbibing the morning dews," said Father Wynn archly, illustrating his metaphor with a movement of his hand to his lips. "What have we here?"

"An anonymous gift," replied Low simply, recognizing the father of Nellie by rising from his chair. "It's a volume I've longed to possess, but never could afford to buy. I cannot imagine who sent it to me."

Wynn was for a moment startled by the thought that this recipient of valuable gifts might have influential friends. But a glance at the bare room, which looked like a camp, and the strange, unconventional garb of its occupant, restored his former convictions. There might be a promise of intelligence, but scarcely of prosperity, in the figure before him.

"Ah! We must not forget that we are watched over in the night season," he said, laying his hand on Low's shoulder, with an illustration of celestial guardianship that would have been impious but for its palpable grotesqueness. "No, sir, we know not what a day may bring forth."

Unfortunately, Low's practical mind did not go beyond a mere human interpretation. It was enough, however, to put a new light in his eye and a faint color in his cheek.

"Could it have been Miss Nellie?" he asked, with half-boyish hesitation.

Mr. Wynn was too much of a Christian not to bow before what appeared to him the purely providential interposition of this suggestion. Seizing it and Low at the same moment, he playfully forced him down again in his chair.

"Ah, you rascal!" he said, with infinite archness; "that's your game, is it? You want to trap poor Father Wynn. You want to make him say 'No.' You want to tempt him to commit himself. No, sir!—never, sir!—no, no!"

Firmly convinced that the present was Nellie's, and that her father only good-humoredly guessed it, the young man's simple, truthful nature was embarrassed. He longed to express his gratitude, but feared to betray the young girl's trust. The Reverend Mr. Wynn speedily relieved his mind.

"No," he continued, bestriding a chair, and familiarly confronting Low over its back. "No, sir—no! And you want me to say 'No,' don't you, regarding the little walks of Nellie and a certain young man in the Carquinez Woods?—ha, ha! You'd like me to say that I knew nothing of the botanizings, and the herb collectings, and the picknickings there—he, he!—you sly dog! Perhaps you'd like to tempt Father Wynn further, and make him swear he knows nothing of his daughter disguising herself in a duster and meeting another young man—isn't it another young man?—all alone, eh? Perhaps you want poor old Father Wynn to say No. No, sir, nothing of the kind ever occurred. Ah, you young rascal!"

Slightly troubled, in spite of Wynn's hearty manner, Low, with his usual directness, however, said, "I do not want anyone to deny that I have seen Miss Nellie."

"Certainly, certainly," said Wynn, abandoning his method, considerably disconcerted by Low's simplicity, and a certain natural reserve that shook off his familiarity. "Certainly it's a noble thing to be able to put your hand on your heart and say to the world, 'Come on, all of you! Observe me; I have nothing to conceal. I walk with Miss Wynn in the woods as her instructor—her teacher, in fact. We cull a flower here and there; we pluck an herb fresh from the hands of the Creator. We look, so to speak, from Nature to Nature's God.' Yes, my young friend, we should be the first to repel the foul calumny that could misinterpret our most innocent actions."

"Calumny?" repeated Low, starting to his feet. "What calumny?"

"My friend, my noble young friend, I recognize your indignation. I know your worth. When I said to Nellie, my only child, my perhaps too simple offspring—a mere wild-flower like yourself—when I said to her, 'Go, my child, walk in the woods with this young man, hand in hand. Let him instruct you from the humblest roots, for he has trodden in the ways of the Almighty. Gather wisdom from his lips, and knowledge from his simple woodman's craft. Make, in fact, a collection not only of herbs, but of moral axioms and experience'—I knew I could trust you, and, trusting you, my young friend, I felt I could trust the world. Perhaps I was weak, foolish. But I thought only of her welfare. I even recall how that to preserve the purity of her garments, I bade her don a simple duster; that, to secure her from the trifling companionship of others, I bade her keep her own counsel, and seek you at seasons known but to yourselves."

"But . . . did Nellie . . . understand you?" interrupted Low hastily.

"I see you read her simple nature. Understand me? No, not at first! Her maidenly instinct—perhaps her duty to another—took the alarm. I remember her words. 'But what will Dunn say?' she asked. 'Will he not be jealous?'"

"Dunn! jealous! I don't understand," said Low, fixing his eyes on Wynn.

"That's just what I said to Nellie. 'Jealous!' I said. 'What, Dunn, your affianced husband, jealous of a mere friend—a teacher, a guide, a philosopher. It is impossible.' Well, sir, she was right. He is jealous. And, more than that, he has imparted his jealousy to others! In other words, he has made a scandal!"

Low's eyes flashed. "Where is your daughter now?" he said sternly.

"At present in bed, suffering from a nervous attack brought on by these unjust suspicions. She appreciates your anxiety, and, knowing that you could not see her, told me to give you this." He handed Low the ring and the letter.

The climax had been forced, and, it must be confessed, was by no means the one Mr. Wynn had fully arranged in his own inner consciousness. He had intended to take an ostentatious leave of Low in the bar-room, deliver the letter with archness, and escape before a possible explosion. He consequently backed towards the door for an emergency. But he was again at fault. That unaffected stoical fortitude in acute suffering, which was the one remaining pride and glory of Low's race, was yet to be revealed to Wynn's civilized eyes.

The young man took the letter, and read it without changing a muscle, folded the ring in it, and dropped it into his haversack. Then he picked up his blanket, threw it over his shoulder, took his trusty rifle in his hand, and turned towards Wynn as if coldly surprised that he was still standing there.

"Are you—are you—going?" stammered Wynn.

"Are you NOT?" replied Low dryly, leaning on his rifle for a moment as if waiting for Wynn to precede him. The preacher looked at him a moment, mumbled something, and then shambled feebly and ineffectively down the staircase before Low, with a painful suggestion to the ordinary observer of being occasionally urged thereto by the moccasin of the young man behind him.

On reaching the lower hall, however, he endeavored to create a diversion in his favor by dashing into the bar-room and clapping the occupants on the back with indiscriminate playfulness. But here again he seemed to be disappointed. To his great discomfiture, a large man not only returned his salutation with powerful levity, but with equal playfulness seized him in his arms, and after an ingenious simulation of depositing him in the horse-trough set him down in affected amazement. "Bleth't if I didn't think from the weight of your hand it wath my old friend, Thacramento Bill," said Curson apologetically, with a wink at the bystanders. "That'th the way Bill alwayth uthed to tackle hith friendth, till he wath one day bounthed by a prithe-fighter in Frithco, whom he had mithtaken for a mithionary." As Mr. Curson's reputation was of a quality that made any form of apology from him instantly acceptable, the amused spectators made way for him as, recognizing Low, who was just leaving the hotel, he turned coolly from them and walked towards him.

"Halloo!" he said, extending his hand. "You're the man I'm waiting for. Did you get a book from the exthpreth offithe latht night?"

"I did. Why?"

"It'th all right. Ath I'm rethponthible for it, I only wanted to know."

"Did YOU send it?" asked Low, quickly fixing his eyes on his face.

"Well, not exactly ME. But it'th not worth making a mythtery of it. Teretha gave me a commithion to buy it and thend it to you anonymouthly. That'th a woman'th nonthenth, for how could thee get a retheipt for it?"

"Then it was HER present," said Low gloomily.

"Of courthe. It wathn't mine, my boy. I'd have thent you a Tharp'th rifle in plathe of that muthle loader you carry, or thomething thenthible. But, I thay! what'th up? You look ath if you had been running all night."

Low grasped his hand. "Thank you," he said hurriedly; "but

it's nothing. Only I must be back to the woods early. Good-by."

But Curson retained Low's hand in his own powerful grip.

"I'll go with you a bit further," he said. "In fact, I've got thomething to thay to you; only don't be in thuch a hurry; the woodth can wait till you get there." Quietly compelling Low to alter his own characteristic Indian stride to keep pace with his, he went on: "I don't mind thaying I rather cottoned to you from the time you acted like a white man—no offenthe—to Teretha. She thayth you were left when a child lying round, jutht ath promithcuouthly ath she wath; and if I can do anything towardth putting you on the trail of your people, I'll do it. I know thome of the voyageurth who traded with the Cherokeeth, and your father wath one-wathn't he?" He glanced at Low's utterly abstracted and immobile face. "I thay, you don't theem to take a hand in thith game, pardner. What'th the row? Ith anything wrong over there?" and he pointed to the Carquinez Woods, which were just looming out of the morning horizon in the distance.

Low stopped. The last words of his companion seemed to recall him to himself. He raised his eyes automatically to the woods and started.

"There IS something wrong over there," he said breathlessly. "Look!"

"I thee nothing," said Curson, beginning to doubt Low's sanity; "nothing more than I thaw an hour ago."

"Look again. Don't you see that smoke rising straight up? It isn't blown over there from the Divide; it's new smoke! The fire is in the woods!"

"I reckon that'th so," muttered Curson, shading his eyes with his hand. "But, hullo! wait a minute! We'll get hortheth. I say!" he shouted, forgetting his lisp in his excitement— "stop!" But Low had already lowered his head and darted forward like an arrow.

In a few moments he had left not only his companion but the last straggling houses of the outskirts far behind him, and had struck out in a long, swinging trot for the disused "cut-off." Already he fancied he heard the note of clamor in Indian Spring, and thought he distinguished the sound of hurrying hoofs on the great highway. But the sunken trail hid it from his view. From the column of smoke now plainly visible in the growing morning light he tried to locate the scene of the conflagration. It was evidently not a fire advancing regularly from the outer skirt of the wood, communicated to it from the Divide; it was a local outburst near its centre. It was not in the direction of his cabin in the tree. There was no immediate danger to Teresa, unless fear drove her beyond the confines of the wood into the hands of those who might recognize her. The screaming of jays and ravens above his head quickened his speed, as it heralded the rapid advance of the flames; and the unexpected apparition of a bounding body, flattened and flying over the yellow plain, told him that even the secure retreat of the mountain wild-cat had been invaded. A sudden recollection of Teresa's uncontrollable terror that first night smote him with remorse and redoubled his efforts. Alone in the track of these frantic and bewildered beasts, to what madness might she not be driven!

The sharp crack of a rifle from the high road turned his course momentarily in that direction. The smoke was curling lazily over the heads of the party of men in the road, while the huge hulk of a grizzly was disappearing in the distance. A battue of the escaping animals had commenced! In the bitterness of his heart he caught at the horrible suggestion, and resolved to save her from them or die with her there.

How fast he ran, or the time it took him to reach the woods, has never been known. Their outlines were already hidden when he entered them. To a sense less keen, a courage less desperate, and a purpose less unaltered than Low's, the wood would have been impenetrable. The central fire was still confined to the lofty tree tops, but the downward rush of wind from time to time drove the smoke into the aisles in blinding and suffocating volumes. To simulate the creeping animals, and fall to the ground on hands and knees, feel his way through the underbrush when the smoke was densest, or take advantage of its momentary lifting, and without uncertainty, mistake, or hesitation glide from tree to tree in one undeviating course, was possible only to an experienced woodsman. To keep his reason and insight so clear as to be able in the midst of this bewildering confusion to shape that course so as to intersect the wild and unknown tract of an inexperienced, frightened wanderer belonged to Low, and Low alone. He was making his way against the wind towards the fire. He had reasoned that she was either in comparative safety to windward of it, or he should meet her being driven towards him by it, or find her succumbed and fainting at its feet. To do this he must penetrate the burning belt, and then pass under the blazing dome. He was already upon it; he could see the falling fire dropping like rain or blown like gorgeous blossoms of the conflagration across his path. The space was lit up brilliantly. The vast shafts of dull copper cast no shadow below, but there was no sign nor token of any human being. For a moment the young man was at fault. It was true this hidden heart of the forest bore no undergrowth; the cool matted carpet of the aisles seemed to quench the glowing fragments as they fell. Escape might be difficult, but not impossible, yet every moment was precious. He leaned against a tree, and sent his voice like a clarion before him: "Teresa!" There was no reply. He called again. A faint cry at his back from the trail he had just traversed made him turn. Only a few paces behind him, blinded and staggering, but following like a beaten and wounded animal, Teresa, halted, knelt, clasped her hands, and dumbly held them out before her. "Teresa!" he cried again, and sprang to her side.

She caught him by the knees, and lifted her face imploringly to his.

"Say that again!" she cried, passionately. "Tell me it was Teresa you called, and no other! You have come back for me! You would not let me die here alone!"

He lifted her tenderly in his arms, and cast a rapid glance around him. It might have been his fancy, but there seemed a dull glow in the direction he had come.

"You do not speak!" she said. "Tell me! You did not come here to seek her?"

"Whom?" he said quickly.

"Nellie!"

With a sharp cry he let her slip to the ground. All the pent-up agony, rage, and mortification of the last hour broke from him in that inarticulate outburst. Then, catching her hands again, he dragged her to his level.

"Hear me!" he cried, disregarding the whirling smoke and the fiery baptism that sprinkled them—"hear me! If you value your life, if you value your soul, and if you do not want me to cast you to the beasts like Jezebel of old, never—never take that accursed name again upon your lips. Seek her—HER? Yes! Seek her to tie her like a witch's daughter of hell to that blazing tree!" He stopped. "Forgive me," he said in a changed voice. "I'm mad, and forgetting myself and you. Come."

Without noticing the expression of half-savage delight that had passed across her face, he lifted her in his arms.

"Which way are you going?" she asked, passing her hands vaguely across his breast, as if to reassure herself of his identity.

"To our camp by the scarred tree," he replied.

"Not there, not there," she said, hurriedly. "I was driven from there just now. I thought the fire began there until I came here."

Then it was as he feared. Obeying the same mysterious law that had launched this fatal fire like a thunderbolt from the burning mountain crest five miles away into the heart of the Carquinez Woods, it had again leaped a mile beyond, and was hemming them between two narrowing lines of fire. But Low was not daunted. Retracing his steps through the blinding smoke, he strode off at right angles to the trail near the point where he had entered the wood. It was the spot where he had first lifted Nellie in his arms to carry her to the hidden spring. If any recollection of it crossed his mind at that moment, it was only shown in his redoubled energy. He did not glide through the thick underbrush, as on that day, but seemed to take a savage pleasure in breaking through it with sheer brute force. Once Teresa insisted upon relieving him of the burden of her weight, but after a few steps she staggered blindly against him, and would fain have recourse once more to his strong arms. And so, alternately staggering, bending, crouching, or bounding and crashing on, but always in one direction, they burst through the jealous rampart, and came upon the sylvan haunt of the hidden spring. The great angle of the half-fallen tree acted as a barrier to the wind and drifting smoke, and the cool spring sparkled and bubbled in the almost translucent air. He laid her down beside the water, and bathed her face and hands. As he did so his quick eye caught sight of a woman's handkerchief lying at the foot of the disrupted root. Dropping Teresa's hand, he walked towards it, and with the toe of his moccasin gave it one vigorous kick into the ooze at the overflow of the spring. He turned to Teresa, but she evidently had not noticed the act.

"Where are you?" she asked, with a smile.

Something in her movement struck him! He came towards her, and bending down looked into her face. "Teresa! Good God!—look at me! What has happened?"

She raised her eyes to his. There was a slight film across them; the lids were blackened; the beautiful lashes gone forever!

"I see you a little now, I think," she said, with a smile, passing her hands vaguely over his face. "It must have happened when he fainted, and I had to drag him through the blazing brush; both my hands were full, and I could not cover my eyes."

"Drag whom?" said Low, quickly.

"Why, Dunn."

"Dunn! He here?" said Low, hoarsely.

"Yes; didn't you read the note I left on the herbarium? Didn't you come to the camp-fire?" she asked hurriedly, clasping his hands. "Tell me quickly!"

"No!"

"Then you were not there—then you didn't leave me to die?"

"No! I swear it, Teresa!" the stoicism that had upheld his own agony breaking down before her strong emotion.

"Thank God!" She threw her arms around him, and hid her aching eyes in his troubled breast.

"Tell me all, Teresa," he whispered in her listening ear. "Don't move; stay there, and tell me all."

With her face buried in his bosom, as if speaking to his heart alone, she told him part, but not all. With her eyes filled with tears, but a smile on her lips, radiant with new-found happiness, she told him how she had overheard the plans of Dunn and Brace, how she had stolen their conveyance to warn him in time. But here she stopped, dreading to say a word that would shatter the hope she was building upon his sudden revulsion of feeling for Nellie. She could not bring herself to repeat their interview—that would come later, when they were safe and out of danger; now not even the secret of his birth must come between them with its distraction, to mar their perfect communion. She faltered that Dunn had fainted from weakness, and that she had dragged him out of danger. "He will never interfere with us—I mean," she said softly, "with ME again. I can promise you that as well as if he had sworn it."

"Let him pass, now," said Low; "that will come later on," he added, unconsciously repeating her thought in a tone that made her heart sick. "But tell me, Teresa, why did you go to Excelsior?"

She buried her head still deeper, as if to hide it. He felt her broken heart beat against his own; he was conscious of a depth of feeling her rival had never awakened in him. The possibility of Teresa loving him had never occurred to his simple nature. He bent his head and kissed her. She was frightened, and unloosed her clinging arms; but he retained her hand, and said, "We will leave this accursed place, and you shall go with me as you said you would; nor need you ever leave me, unless you wish it."

She could hear the beating of her own heart through his words; she longed to look at the eyes and lips that told her this, and read the meaning his voice alone could not entirely convey. For the first time she felt the loss of her sight. She did not know that it was, in this moment of happiness, the last blessing vouchsafed to her miserable life.

A few moments of silence followed, broken only by the distant rumor of the conflagration and the crash of falling boughs.

"It may be an hour yet," he whispered, "before the fire has swept a path for us to the road below. We are safe here, unless some sudden current should draw the fire down upon us. You are not frightened?" She pressed his hand; she was thinking of the pale face of Dunn, lying in the secure retreat she had purchased for him at such a sacrifice. Yet the possibility of danger to him now for a moment marred her present happiness and security. "You think the fire will not go north of where you found me?" she asked softly.

"I think not," he said, "but I will reconnoitre. Stay where you are."

They pressed hands, and parted. He leaped upon the slanting trunk and ascended it rapidly. She waited in mute expectation.

There was a sudden movement of the root on which she sat, a deafening crash, and she was thrown forward on her face.

The vast bulk of the leaning tree, dislodged from its aerial support by the gradual sapping of the spring at its roots, or by the crumbling of the bark from the heat, had slipped, made a half revolution, and, falling, overbore the lesser trees in its path, and tore, in its resistless momentum, a broad opening to the underbrush.

With a cry to Low, Teresa staggered to her feet. There was an interval of hideous silence, but no reply. She called again. There was a sudden deepening roar, the blast of a fiery furnace swept through the opening, a thousand luminous points around her burst into fire, and in an instant she was lost in a whirlwind of smoke and flame! From the onset of its fury to its culmination twenty minutes did not elapse; but in that interval a radius of two hundred yards around the hidden spring was swept of life and light and motion.

For the rest of that day and part of the night a pall of smoke hung above the scene of desolation. It lifted only towards the morning, when the moon, rising high, picked out in black and silver the shrunken and silent columns of those roofless vaults, shorn of base and capital. It flickered on the still, overflowing pool of the hidden spring, and shone upon the white face of Low, who, with a rootlet of the fallen tree holding him down like an arm across his breast, seemed to be sleeping peacefully in the sleeping water.

* * * * *

Contemporaneous history touched him as briefly, but not as gently. "It is now definitely ascertained," said "The Slumgullion Mirror," "that Sheriff Dunn met his fate in the Carquinez Woods in the performance of his duty; that fearless man having received information of the concealment of a band of horse thieves in their recesses. The desperadoes are presumed to have escaped, as the only remains found are those of two wretched tramps, one of whom is said to have been a digger, who supported himself upon roots and herbs, and the other a degraded half-white woman. It is not unreasonable to suppose that the fire originated through their carelessness, although Father Wynn of the First Baptist Church, in his powerful discourse of last Sunday, pointed at the warning and lesson of such catastrophes. It may not be out of place here to say that the rumors regarding an engagement between the pastor's accomplished daughter and the late lamented sheriff are utterly without foundation, as it has been an on dit for some time in all well-informed circles that the indefatigable Mr. Brace, of Wells, Fargo and Co.'s Express, will shortly lead the lady to the hymeneal altar."

ABOUT THE AUTHOR

 **Francis Bret Harte** (August 25, 1836–May 6, 1902) was an American author and poet, best remembered for his accounts of pioneering life in California.

Born in Albany, New York, Harte moved to California in 1853, later working there in a number of capacities, including miner, teacher, messenger, and journalist. He spent part of his life in the northern California coast town now known as Arcata, at the time it was just a mining camp on Humboldt Bay.

His first literary efforts, including poetry and prose, appeared in The Californian, an early literary journal edited by Charles Henry Webb. In 1868 he became editor of The Overland Monthly, another new literary magazine, but this one more in tune with the pioneering spirit of excitement in California. His story, "The Luck of Roaring Camp," appeared in the magazine's second edition, propelling Harte to nationwide fame.

As an established literary figure, he was appointed to the position of United States Consul in the town of Krefeld, Germany in 1878 and Glasgow in 1880. In 1885 he settled in London. During the thirty years he spent in Europe, he never abandoned writing, and maintained a prodigious output of stories that retained the freshness of his earlier work. He died in England in 1902.

Choose from Thousands of 1stWorldLibrary Classics By

A. M. Barnard
Ada Leverson
Adolphus William Ward
Aesop
Agatha Christie
Alexander Aaronsohn
Alexander Kielland
Alexandre Dumas
Alfred Gatty
Alfred Ollivant
Alice Duer Miller
Alice Turner Curtis
Alice Dunbar
Allen Chapman
Alleyne Ireland
Ambrose Bierce
Amelia E. Barr
Amory H. Bradford
Andrew Lang
Andrew McFarland Davis
Andy Adams
Angela Brazil
Anna Alice Chapin
Anna Sewell
Annie Besant
Annie Hamilton Donnell
Annie Payson Call
Annie Roe Carr
Annonaymous
Anton Chekhov
Archibald Lee Fletcher
Arnold Bennett
Arthur C. Benson
Arthur Conan Doyle
Arthur M. Winfield
Arthur Ransome
Arthur Schnitzler
Arthur Train
Atticus
B.H. Baden-Powell
B. M. Bower
B. C. Chatterjee
Baroness Emmuska Orczy
Baroness Orczy
Basil King
Bayard Taylor
Ben Macomber
Bertha Muzzy Bower
Bjornstjerne Bjornson

Booth Tarkington
Boyd Cable
Bram Stoker
C. Collodi
C. E. Orr
C. M. Ingleby
Carolyn Wells
Catherine Parr Traill
Charles A. Eastman
Charles Amory Beach
Charles Dickens
Charles Dudley Warner
Charles Farrar Browne
Charles Ives
Charles Kingsley
Charles Klein
Charles Hanson Towne
Charles Lathrop Pack
Charles Romyn Dake
Charles Whibley
Charles Willing Beale
Charlotte M. Braeme
Charlotte M. Yonge
Charlotte Perkins Stetson
Clair W. Hayes
Clarence Day Jr.
Clarence E. Mulford
Clemence Housman
Confucius
Coningsby Dawson
Cornelis DeWitt Wilcox
Cyril Burleigh
D. H. Lawrence
Daniel Defoe
David Garnett
Dinah Craik
Don Carlos Janes
Donald Keyhoe
Dorothy Kilner
Dougan Clark
Douglas Fairbanks
E. Nesbit
E. P. Roe
E. Phillips Oppenheim
E. S. Brooks
Earl Barnes
Edgar Rice Burroughs
Edith Van Dyne
Edith Wharton

Edward Everett Hale
Edward J. O'Biren
Edward S. Ellis
Edwin L. Arnold
Eleanor Atkins
Eleanor Hallowell Abbott
Eliot Gregory
Elizabeth Gaskell
Elizabeth McCracken
Elizabeth Von Arnim
Ellem Key
Emerson Hough
Emilie F. Carlen
Emily Bronte
Emily Dickinson
Enid Bagnold
Enilor Macartney Lane
Erasmus W. Jones
Ernie Howard Pie
Ethel May Dell
Ethel Turner
Ethel Watts Mumford
Eugene Sue
Eugenie Foa
Eugene Wood
Eustace Hale Ball
Evelyn Everett-green
Everard Cotes
F. H. Cheley
F. J. Cross
F. Marion Crawford
Fannie E. Newberry
Federick Austin Ogg
Ferdinand Ossendowski
Fergus Hume
Florence A. Kilpatrick
Fremont B. Deering
Francis Bacon
Francis Darwin
Frances Hodgson Burnett
Frances Parkinson Keyes
Frank Gee Patchin
Frank Harris
Frank Jewett Mather
Frank L. Packard
Frank V. Webster
Frederic Stewart Isham
Frederick Trevor Hill
Frederick Winslow Taylor

Friedrich Kerst
Friedrich Nietzsche
Fyodor Dostoyevsky
G.A. Henty
G.K. Chesterton
Gabrielle E. Jackson
Garrett P. Serviss
Gaston Leroux
George A. Warren
George Ade
Geroge Bernard Shaw
George Cary Eggleston
George Durston
George Ebers
George Eliot
George Gissing
George MacDonald
George Meredith
George Orwell
George Sylvester Viereck
George Tucker
George W. Cable
George Wharton James
Gertrude Atherton
Gordon Casserly
Grace E. King
Grace Gallatin
Grace Greenwood
Grant Allen
Guillermo A. Sherwell
Gulielma Zollinger
Gustav Flaubert
H. A. Cody
H. B. Irving
H.C. Bailey
H. G. Wells
H. H. Munro
H. Irving Hancock
H. R. Naylor
H. Rider Haggard
H. W. C. Davis
Haldeman Julius
Hall Caine
Hamilton Wright Mabie
Hans Christian Andersen
Harold Avery
Harold McGrath
Harriet Beecher Stowe
Harry Castlemon
Harry Coghill
Harry Houidini

Hayden Carruth
Helent Hunt Jackson
Helen Nicolay
Hendrik Conscience
Hendy David Thoreau
Henri Barbusse
Henrik Ibsen
Henry Adams
Henry Ford
Henry Frost
Henry James
Henry Jones Ford
Henry Seton Merriman
Henry W Longfellow
Herbert A. Giles
Herbert Carter
Herbert N. Casson
Herman Hesse
Hildegard G. Frey
Homer
Honore De Balzac
Horace B. Day
Horace Walpole
Horatio Alger Jr.
Howard Pyle
Howard R. Garis
Hugh Lofting
Hugh Walpole
Humphry Ward
Ian Maclaren
Inez Haynes Gillmore
Irving Bacheller
Isabel Cecilia Williams
Isabel Hornibrook
Israel Abrahams
Ivan Turgenev
J.G.Austin
J. Henri Fabre
J. M. Barrie
J. M. Walsh
J. Macdonald Oxley
J. R. Miller
J. S. Fletcher
J. S. Knowles
J. Storer Clouston
J. W. Duffield
Jack London
Jacob Abbott
James Allen
James Andrews
James Baldwin

James Branch Cabell
James DeMille
James Joyce
James Lane Allen
James Lane Allen
James Oliver Curwood
James Oppenheim
James Otis
James R. Driscoll
Jane Abbott
Jane Austen
Jane L. Stewart
Janet Aldridge
Jens Peter Jacobsen
Jerome K. Jerome
Jessie Graham Flower
John Buchan
John Burroughs
John Cournos
John F. Kennedy
John Gay
John Glasworthy
John Habberton
John Joy Bell
John Kendrick Bangs
John Milton
John Philip Sousa
John Taintor Foote
Jonas Lauritz Idemil Lie
Jonathan Swift
Joseph A. Altsheler
Joseph Carey
Joseph Conrad
Joseph E. Badger Jr
Joseph Hergesheimer
Joseph Jacobs
Jules Vernes
Julian Hawthrone
Julie A Lippmann
Justin Huntly McCarthy
Kakuzo Okakura
Karle Wilson Baker
Kate Chopin
Kenneth Grahame
Kenneth McGaffey
Kate Langley Bosher
Kate Langley Bosher
Katherine Cecil Thurston
Katherine Stokes
L. A. Abbot
L. T. Meade

L. Frank Baum
Latta Griswold
Laura Dent Crane
Laura Lee Hope
Laurence Housman
Lawrence Beasley
Leo Tolstoy
Leonid Andreyev
Lewis Carroll
Lewis Sperry Chafer
Lilian Bell
Lloyd Osbourne
Louis Hughes
Louis Joseph Vance
Louis Tracy
Louisa May Alcott
Lucy Fitch Perkins
Lucy Maud Montgomery
Luther Benson
Lydia Miller Middleton
Lyndon Orr
M. Corvus
M. H. Adams
Margaret E. Sangster
Margret Howth
Margaret Vandercook
Margaret W. Hungerford
Margret Penrose
Maria Edgeworth
Maria Thompson Daviess
Mariano Azuela
Marion Polk Angellotti
Mark Overton
Mark Twain
Mary Austin
Mary Catherine Crowley
Mary Cole
Mary Hastings Bradley
Mary Roberts Rinehart
Mary Rowlandson
M. Wollstonecraft Shelley
Maud Lindsay
Max Beerbohm
Myra Kelly
Nathaniel Hawthrone
Nicolo Machiavelli
O. F. Walton
Oscar Wilde

Owen Johnson
P.G. Wodehouse
Paul and Mabel Thorne
Paul G. Tomlinson
Paul Severing
Percy Brebner
Percy Keese Fitzhugh
Peter B. Kyne
Plato
Quincy Allen
R. Derby Holmes
R. L. Stevenson
R. S. Ball
Rabindranath Tagore
Rahul Alvares
Ralph Bonehill
Ralph Henry Barbour
Ralph Victor
Ralph Waldo Emmerson
Rene Descartes
Ray Cummings
Rex Beach
Rex E. Beach
Richard Harding Davis
Richard Jefferies
Richard Le Gallienne
Robert Barr
Robert Frost
Robert Gordon Anderson
Robert L. Drake
Robert Lansing
Robert Lynd
Robert Michael Ballantyne
Robert W. Chambers
Rosa Nouchette Carey
Rudyard Kipling
Saint Augustine
Samuel B. Allison
Samuel Hopkins Adams
Sarah Bernhardt
Sarah C. Hallowell
Selma Lagerlof
Sherwood Anderson
Sigmund Freud
Standish O'Grady
Stanley Weyman
Stella Benson
Stella M. Francis

Stephen Crane
Stewart Edward White
Stijn Streuvels
Swami Abhedananda
Swami Parmananda
T. S. Ackland
T. S. Arthur
The Princess Der Ling
Thomas A. Janvier
Thomas A Kempis
Thomas Anderton
Thomas Bailey Aldrich
Thomas Bulfinch
Thomas De Quincey
Thomas Dixon
Thomas H. Huxley
Thomas Hardy
Thomas More
Thornton W. Burgess
U. S. Grant
Upton Sinclair
Valentine Williams
Various Authors
Vaughan Kester
Victor Appleton
Victor G. Durham
Victoria Cross
Virginia Woolf
Wadsworth Camp
Walter Camp
Walter Scott
Washington Irving
Wilbur Lawton
Wilkie Collins
Willa Cather
Willard F. Baker
William Dean Howells
William le Queux
W. Makepeace Thackeray
William W. Walter
William Shakespeare
Winston Churchill
Yei Theodora Ozaki
Yogi Ramacharaka
Young E. Allison
Zane Grey